THE BADER WING

THE BADER WING

John Frayn Turner

WRENS PARK

First published in the UK in 1981 by Midas Books

This edition published 1999 by Wrens Park Publishing, an imprint of
W. J. Williams & Son Ltd

British Library Cataloguing-in-Publication Data
A catalogue record for this book
is available from the British Library

ISBN 0905 778 41 3

Printed in England by St Edmundsbury Press Ltd, Bury St Edmunds, Suffolk

Contents

Preface

This is the first book to deal exclusively with 12 Group and its crucial contribution to the Battle of Britain. These squadrons were based entirely north of the Thames and led by the legendary Douglas Bader. Other accounts have included their part in the overall fight, while some have been less than fair to 12 Group in the Big Wing controversy that has surrounded its activities for forty years.

To tell this inspiring story, I have had access to every original log of every single sortie by every pilot in 12 Group. As well as studying these thousand or so reports, I have also of course seen the broader records of both 11 and 12 Groups and Fighter Command itself. In this way I have tried to piece together a comprehensive version of the Big Wing in its relation to the Battle of Britain. I feel that the facts presented by assembling this aerial jigsaw speak for themselves — and more eloquently than any theories. The Big Wing worked.

Douglas Bader was the legless leader of this unique five-squadron wing. I knew him for a number of years and feel fortunate to have been able to count him as a friend. I am well aware that he would have wished to 'distance' himself from any sort of subjective controversy about the Big Wing, and he would also have insisted on giving fullest honour to the many pilots who flew with him in 1940 and 1941. However, I hope that my view of the events portrayed in this book accord more or less with his own feelings about those unrepeatable days.

I am very grateful to the distinguished pilots whose exclusive comments on Bader are quoted here: Johnnie Johnson, Peter Townsend, Laddie Lucas, Sholto Douglas, Peter Brothers, Hugh Dundas and Alan Deere. I would also like to thank William Collins for permission to reprint the brief but telling extract by Paul Brickhill from 'Reach for the Sky'. Apart from that, I must accept responsibility for the rest of the text.

One final note: the contemporary claims of success made during the battle are now of course known to have been exaggerated.

John Frayn Turner
February 1990.

Prologue

On 14th December 1931, Douglas Bader was about to face the need to come to grips with life for the first time. He was twenty-one years old and flying Bulldogs as a Royal Air Force pilot officer in 23 Squadron at Kenley, Surrey. Douglas flew over to Woodley Aerodrome, Reading, with a couple of other pilots, Phillips and Richardson, in their three Bulldogs to see Phillips' brother there. They had coffee and chatted to some of the chaps in the flying club at Woodley. One or two of them had been trying to needle Douglas into showing them some aerobatics, but the RAF pilots were under orders not to do so. Douglas had taken part in the Hendon Air Display as part of the Gamecocks aerobatic team.

The trio took off in their Bulldogs to fly back to Kenley. Phillips and Richardson went first, while Douglas brought up the rear. He was still thinking of this needling in the clubhouse and decided to show them what he could do. He turned, dived low over Woodley field and did a slow roll a few feet off the ground. He made a slight mistake with his Bulldog, which crashed on to the grass somewhere in the middle of the airfield. Douglas finished up with the whole aeroplane wrapped around him.

He was not dead. He was not even unconscious. But he had hurt himself very badly. His right leg had the rudder bar right through the knee and was very nearly severed from his body. His left leg was broken between the knee and the ankle where the seat had been faced forward and he was still sort of sitting on it. The strange thing was that he did not seem to be feeling any particular pain in this messy lower part of his crushed body. Douglas was of course wearing his usual flying overalls and uniform, so the evidence of the crash was not yet apparent, but all tangled up in his clothing. The pain that he did in fact feel came from his back. The fighting harness had held him back when the aeroplane hit the ground and his body had tried to lurch forward. This harness saved his life and he felt the pain from the wrench to prove it. At that first minute after impact, Douglas simply sensed a kind of buzzing in both his legs, rather like the feeling you get when hitting your funny-bone. Only this was in his legs.

Douglas and the aeroplane finally landed upright and did not catch fire. A man called Cruttenden got to the Bulldog first, undid the straps, somehow dragged Douglas out of the cockpit, and transferred him to an ambulance that had arrived with commendable speed. Cruttenden sat with him in the ambulance and saw that he was bleeding dangerously from his right leg. Douglas had severed the artery and so Cruttenden stuck a large hand tightly over the bit of overall and leg where it was all emerging. Douglas is convinced that Cruttenden saved his life by that action alone.

They hurried him to the Royal Berkshire Hospital at Reading, where the next thing he remembered was lying on or near the operating table, with the face of the splendid anaesthetist, Commander Parry Price, gazing down at him. Price was about to put the nozzle over Douglas's face, when he protested as vehemently as he could:

'Don't give me an anaesthetic–I can't stand those things.'

The reason for this outburst was because Douglas had been taken to a nursing home in Manchester Square, London, by his mother when he was only about five and a half. Here he had been pushed on to an operating table, preparatory to having his tonsils or adenoids out. They told him he had been dressed in a red nightshirt so that he would not see the blood–hardly good psychology! Then someone thrust a great nozzle over his face. This had stuck in Douglas's mind for sixteen years and was why he tried to push the nozzle away then.

That was all Douglas recalled for a day or two.

Eventually the world filtered back into his consciousness. He opened his eyes and made out the figure of a sister, with her back towards him. She was standing in front of a window and looking out at a blue sky, with scraps of clouds fluffing across the sun. Douglas could not remember anything, neither his name nor what had happened. His head lay against the inner wall and his feet pointed towards that window. Then looking again, he saw a cradle over his legs. He looked beyond that to the end of the bed, to the nurse, to the sky beyond.

'What am I doing here?' he said.

'You're awake, are you? Well, you've had an accident in an aeroplane and you've hurt yourself. We're looking after you.'

'Thanks awfully.'

Douglas gradually got his mind operating again and thought to himself. 'I must have hurt my legs—as there's a cradle over the bed.'

The sister left the room and returned with a man wearing a grey herringbone suit. He had slightly grey, wavy hair and looked rather like a don or something academic.

'I'm afraid you've had a bit of an accident, old son, and we've had to take your right leg off,' he said.

Douglas was extremely weak, too much so to care. This initial statement made no real impact on him at all. All he said was 'I'm sorry, doctor, I'm being such a nuisance.' The doctor was in fact the surgeon, Leonard Joyce, who had performed this first operation. Douglas was not too weak, however, to have a look underneath the bedclothes as soon as he was left alone again. He wanted to see what a 'leg off' looked like. He lifted up the bedding slightly and saw that his right leg appeared to be just what he would have expected: a little bit of stump with a bloody bandage around it. Yet it had no effect on him. He did not feel any emotion at all. This was nature helping him over the first shock. He was really too weak to care. Then nature came to the rescue again.

An hour or two after awakening, he started to feel the pain. His left leg began to hurt like hell, but his right leg or the remains of it did not trouble him at all. He learned later that there must have been pain in both, but in such cases the major pain always prevails over the lesser one. Douglas found it hard to tell why this left leg was hurting, because as far as he knew then, it was simply broken and they had set it. When he saw it was still apparently whole, he could not think why the pain was so strong. What he did not realise was that it became badly poisoned.

Not long afterwards, the doctor came back and said: 'Look, we've got to reset that left leg. It's going to hurt a bit, so we're going to give you an anaesthetic.' Another bloody anaesthetic! Then Parry Price came breezing in, wearing one of his broad check suits. He was a great character. He asked Douglas: 'How much do you weigh?'

Douglas replied: 'I used to weigh 11 stones 6 pounds—the exact weight I boxed at as a middleweight.'

'That's fine—now don't worry.'

In due course a nurse appeared with a phial of evil-looking pink fluid! She inserted it in his backside and before he hardly had time to say, 'That's never going to do anything,' Douglas had passed out again.

He woke up feeling very drowsy, but not at all sick and with no other ill effects. His left leg was still hurting like hell, though. Just as it had been before. He started to think 'I don't know why they don't cut this one off as well.' He was really getting round to that stage, whether feeling seriously or not. He went on lying there in this frame of mind, when the squadron leader of 23 Squadron came in to see him. Douglas realised later that he had probably been sent in for the job. They talked for a bit.

'You know,' Douglas said, 'this bloody left leg hurts like hell. I can't think why they don't cut it off. Because the other one doesn't hurt me at all.'

'Do you really want it to be cut off?' the Squadron leader asked.

'Yes—I just can't wait.'

'Well,' the Squadron leader said, 'as a matter of fact, they have cut it off.'

Douglas only paused for a second.

'Then why the hell does it hurt so much? Surely it shouldn't do now?'

He did not even bother to look at it to check up. He was primarily concerned at the fact that it still hurt him. Fortunately there is nothing so effective as pain to make someone concentrate their attention. At least the pain occupied Douglas's mind to the exclusion of everything else. So perhaps it was a good thing just at that time.

During this twilight period after he had lost his second leg, Douglas touched bottom. The pain went on and on and he felt weaker instead of stronger. He got to the stage of being slightly lightheaded and not really aware of what was going on around him. Shadowy figures came and went and did things. Douglas felt dimly aware of them. Then the pain started to subside. But so did he. At one time he remembered lying back and feeling no pain of any kind. He did not know if it were night or day even, because he was unaware of any distinctions of time. He was barely conscious of touching or feeling the bed; in fact he was barely conscious at all. But he did vaguely feel that this was marvellous. No pain, no effort, very cosy, very agreeable. Peaceful. Then he heard a slight sound, a murmur, followed by somebody saying:

'Sh! There's a boy dying in there.'

It reached his brain with a clarity and an intensity, as though someone had said the words right beside his bed. He suddenly got a jerk in his system and he reacted. 'So that's why it's so cosy. So that's what they think. Well, they're bloody well wrong. I'm going to do something about this.' Douglas dragged himself into clear consciousness, back came the pain, and he knew he was fighting it. He started slowly to get better.

Later on this left him with a complete indifference to death. He was unafraid of it, because after that it did not occur to him that it was anything other than rather agreeable. He has never been specifically frightened of death since that incident. But this did not alter his resolve to avoid it at that time of his life. At twenty-one he had a lot left to do.

People have often asked Douglas, 'Wasn't it a terrible shock when you realised you had lost both your legs?' The answer was 'No, because I never had any shock.' He had been cushioned against any idea of a shock by the persistent repetition of hearing that he had had his legs off. It ceased to have any impact and he became rather bored by the whole thing. And strangely enough, Douglas derived strength and mental balance from the very knowledge that it had been his own fault.

As he recovered after that critical point, Douglas began to spend a lot of his time in reading. He has always loved poetry and he re-read Swinburne while in hospital.

> 'The glass of the years is brittle
> wherein we gaze for a span.'

Only a few days or weeks earlier, he had been a healthy, athletic young man without any cares. Suddenly the brittle glass had shattered and he was lying in bed minus his legs and reading Swinburne. He went on combating the pain, which lessened the impact of the loss of his legs. By the time he could eventually assimilate the significance of his accident, its importance had already diminished. The pain plus the repetition of the fact did this. The result was that the absence of impact had a considerable effect on his mental attitude to the whole affair and his own future. So when the pain did end, and he began to mend physically, the mind was not agitated by the loss of legs. This was because Douglas had no idea of life without legs, could not assess the future, so left it alone. Each day was enough. Later on, in fact, when he was recuperating, Douglas used to dream he had artificial legs, but they worked in exactly the same way as his ordinary legs. This was because he had never known artificial legs or being without his real ones, so that anything in his subconscious was automatically associated with what he could do before he had lost them.

On Christmas Eve 1931, they moved him across to the nursing home called Greenlands. He was well looked after here and thoroughly spoiled. In general he had a splendid time in this early convalescence.

A man came over from Oxford to fit him with a peg leg. The way they fitted him was to wrap some wet plaster of paris bandage around his leg, let it set, and then rip it off. Douglas's leg was pretty sore, because the stump had not healed completely. What they seemed to have forgotten was that when the plaster of paris came off—so did all the hairs! This made Douglas shout with rage. The whole impression came off, with all the hairs of his upper leg stuck inside it!

The man returned with a peg leg with a hinge to look after the bend and stretch of the knee. He also brought a corset. The peg leg had a rubber heel stop on the bottom. Douglas put on the peg leg and tried to get up on some crutches. He was still very feeble after a couple of months' complete inactivity, apart from the major shock to the system of losing the legs. He did not do well in supporting himself and the crutches kept flying out in all directions. The nurse, Dorothy Brace, was wonderful with him, but said, 'Take it easy—and I do wish you wouldn't use that appalling language!' But after a couple of days, Douglas managed to get upright on the peg leg, with the aid of the crutches, and he staggered about for a few steps. Soon he improved and was hopping around freely on this leg.

So Douglas had quite a bit of fun walking about successfully on his peg leg progressing from the high crutches down to elbow crutches. Then the surgeon, Leonard Joyce, told him, 'I've got to have another go at both your legs, because they were both what we call guillotine operations and I haven't had a chance to trim them properly, so that the artificial leg people can make a decent job.' The bone on Douglas's right leg was almost sticking through the flesh, while the fibula on his left leg was too long.

'I'll have to do you again,' he told Douglas, 'but I'll do them both together. Then you'll be in good condition to go to the artificial leg place.' He gave Douglas the greatest confidence and was a remarkable surgeon for those days. So Douglas had his legs trimmed up, which was followed by yet another period of pain and inconvenience.

Then came the time to leave Greenlands. It was a wrench for Douglas, but he kissed all the nurses, got into a Royal Air Force car, and was taken to the RAF Hospital at Uxbridge. They had all minded so much at Greenlands. Douglas would not forget them.

But at Uxbridge he felt he was back in an atmosphere he really understood and where he really belonged. There were rules and regulations, yet they were reasonable ones. Douglas was in a ward with other officers. Legend has it that one of them had had his ear drop off during a guest night at RAF Martlesham! He was at Uxbridge to have it riveted back on again! Victor Streatfield had broken his arm. John Peel had broken his leg. The whole RAF atmosphere had a bracing effect on Douglas! He used to go around on his peg leg or sometimes early on, with his wheelchair, and he would end up in a flower bed with the chair on top of him. This all helped to restore his sense of humour. One of the many RAF traditions has always been to make light of whatever happens: to minimise it whether good or bad.

Meanwhile, with the natural optimism of youth allied to Douglas's own individual joie de vivre, he had the feeling that if someone would just give him some proper artificial legs, he would be running around on them in no time flat. Only in this context, the operative word was in fact, flat. He went to Roehampton, where he was fitted with proper legs. These had a foot on them below the knee and an artificial articulated leg above the knee. But there was no physiotherapy in those days. He had a terrible job trying to manipulate the upper leg. He got this pair of legs and took them back to Uxbridge. For the first time since his accident, he received its full impact. He found himself utterly unable to move. To walk on these things seemed totally impossible. This was no moment for a philosophical approach to the problem. It became a straight physical battle. Douglas refused to accept this unexpected setback. He decided he was not going to be a nuisance or a burden to his friends, that he would become independent of the assistance of other people. That was his immediate and only goal.

He tried to walk up the ward. He fell down. Needless to say, it was a linoleum floor and a highly polished one at that. Douglas picked himself up and tried again. He fell again. He kept on falling. The chaps in the ward encouraged him, lifted him off the ground, or else just laughed at him. They were in fact behaving naturally and characteristically, and nothing could have been better calculated to help him. They made rude remarks about his efforts, but they picked him up. Gradually he got better at standing and walking . . .

CHAPTER 1

Bader's First Victory

This is a true story of the Battle of Britain. The story of a man, a squadron, a wing and a group: Douglas Bader, 242 Squadron, The Bader Wing, 12 Group. When the Battle of Britain began, Bader was a squadron leader in command of the Canadian 242 Squadron. This formed part of 12 Group, Fighter Command, covering an area somewhere north of the River Thames approximately to East Anglia. Mainly south of the Thames was the fighter force of 11 Group in South-East England, while 10 Group were responsible for the region further West.

The various commanders involved were as follows: Air Chief Marshal Sir Hugh C T Dowding was the Air Officer Commanding-in-Chief, Fighter Command, whose headquarters were at Bentley Priory, Stanmore, Middlesex; Air Vice-Marshal K R Park was A O C 11 Group; Air Vice-Marshal T L Leigh-Mallory A O C 12 Group; and Air Vice-Marshal Sir C J G Brand A O C 10 Group. The first three of these four commanders will figure vitally in this story just a little later on.

Although many historians may mark the beginning of the Battle of Britain from either mid-July or early-August 1940, the aerial diary really dates from June—even from the drama of Dunkirk. After furious fighting in the skies surrounding Dunkirk, the immortal evacuation was accomplished and 335,000 were brought home safely to English shores.

Within 48 hours of Dunkirk, during the night of 5–6 June, the Germans started air activity over Britain—surely a good reason for calling this the real beginning of the Battle of Britain. By a coincidence, the date of 6 June was precisely four years before D-Day and the invasion of Europe. But on this particular night the enemy attacks were directed against East Coast aerodromes and ports—in the 12 Group area. Bombs fell near Bircham Newton and Horsham St Faith. A dozen high explosives also disrupted the aerodrome at

Hemswell, one hitting a hangar. A few bombs also exploded at the Alexandra Docks in Grimsby.

On the very next night, too, bombs were reported near four aerodromes of Upwood, Cranwell, Mildenhall and Feltwell—all famous names in RAF annals. On one occasion at least, an enemy bomber followed our own bombers back towards the aerodrome and then attacked it. Elsewhere a stray bomb fell on the roof of the United Steel Rolling Mill, Scunthorpe, and another on John Brown's works, but neither of those did much damage. Then on the next night of 7–8 June, East Anglian and Lincolnshire aerodromes again seemed to be the main targets. 12 Group received reports of bombs around half a dozen airfields: Mildenhall, Bircham Newton, Cottesmore, Scunthorpe, Peterborough and King's Lynn. One of the first enemy casualties in this part of the country occurred when a German aircraft crashed at 01.49 hours near Eyke, three miles from Woodbridge. But aerial activity was still all on a very restricted scale by comparison with what was to come.

But by 18–19 June hostile activity reached considerable strength and during that night areas around Scunthorpe, King's Lynn, Waddington and Louth all received bombs. But the enemy suffered several casualties, due to co-operation between searchlights and British fighters. In fact this date marked the start of 12 Group's close encounter with the Luftwaffe. The claim was 5 Heinkel 111s shot down, with two more probably not able to reach their home base. Just after the enemy shot down one of our Blenheims piloted by Sgt Close, Flight Lieutenant Duke-Woolley of 23 Squadron destroyed this self-same Heinkel 111, which crashed near Sheringham. Meanwhile Squadron Leader O'Brien of the same squadron also attacked a Heinkel 111, over Newmarket racecourse region, damaging it severely. But the conflict was not one-sided, for Squadron Leader O'Brien had to bale out, though his navigator and air gunner were both killed. F/O Barnwell and P/O Humphries of 29 Squadron both shot down Heinkel 111s, the enemy aircraft churning up the North Sea off Felixstowe. But F/O Barnwell was reported missing. F/O Ball of 19 Squadron went for a Heinkel 111 near Colchester, riddled it, and the enemy finally crashed as far away as Margate. F/O Petre also of 19 Squadron shot down a Heinkel 111 quite near Cambridge, but he had to bale out after being hit. Badly burned, he was hurried to hospital at Bury St Edmunds.

During the day of 19 June, two or three raiders crossed the East Coast at about 18.00 hours. One of these was actually intercepted out to sea by 66 Squadron, Blue Section. The three fighters comprising the section expended all their ammunition on this Junkers 88, which they last saw in distinct distress only 20 feet from the water.

A matter of hours later after dark, a large force of hostile aircraft were detected in 12 Group area. Most of the raiders operated around the Humber region, probably because the weather conditions further south deteriorated quickly. Some of the raiders were definitely minelaying in the vital Humber zone, but both high explosive and incendiary bombs fell near Louth, Grimsby, Withernsea, Hemswell and Scunthorpe. Several of the enemy raiders were picked out and clearly illuminated by searchlights, two being shot down. S/Ldr Mermagen and P/O Vigors of 222 Squadron were responsible for these Heinkel 111s. So the build-up of enemy was beginning—but slowly.

A couple of nights later on 21–22 June, heavier enemy thrusts were represented by about one hundred hostile aircraft on the table. Aerodromes and towns seemed to be targets: aerodromes in Norfolk, Suffolk and Lincolnshire, and the towns of Grimsby, Hull and Lowestoft. Cloud conditions prevented the searchlights from picking up any of the enemy bombers and although air patrols were in fact flown, no contact could be made. Bombs were reported in a dozen areas: Harleston, Wattisham (from where I later flew at 1500 mph!), Colchester, Bircham Newton, Coltishall, Newmarket, Harwich, Orfordness, Digby, Duxford, Wittering and Winterton. As well as bombing the environs of Louth, the enemy also machine-gunned searchlights. The beam of a searchlight always made the ground crew vulnerable to this sort of attack. And apart from bombing around Grimsby and Hull, the enemy laid mines off the coast and in the Humber estuary.

While all this was going on, Douglas Bader prepared 242 Squadron for future action—and on 24 June reported the squadron operational at Coltishall. He would have to wait another fortnight for his first encounters . . . Meanwhile it is worth sketching in the aerial activity of those next two weeks to illustrate the inevitability of the build-up towards the more momentous days of August and September.

That same night that Bader became operational by day, some 70 enemy aircraft were plotted, though thick cloud precluded any interceptions. A slight switch of targets made East Anglian aerodromes and Midland industrial areas the main recipients. For the first time one or two bigger towns and cities began to be mentioned among the places visited: Derby, Coventry, Debden, Duxford, Coltishall, Bircham Newton, Finningley, Swinderby, Stamford, Lowestoft, Cromer, Wittering and Sutton Bridge.

For the following 24 hours, activity was once more restricted to night-time. The enemy aimed for aerodromes in East Anglia. Grimsby and Hull had some bombs, while several isolated raids penetrated to the Midland industrial areas. Night fighting was still at a relatively primitive stage, but air patrols fared a bit better this time on 25–26 June. P/O Morgan of 222 Squadron actually shot down a Heinkel 111, though he himself sustained severe injuries when his own aircraft crashed afterwards. Several of the enemy bombers were hit fatally by anti aircraft guns firing heavily in the Humber region. Rugby and Wolverhampton figured among the ten locations where bombs fell.

Another night and only a score or so enemy raiders were plotted in 12 Group. Low cloud base interfered with any attempt at contact by RAF fighters and even searchlights failed to find the enemy —the clouds preventing any piercing or penetration by their beams. Two fighters had to force-land during their attempt at interception, but the crews did not sustain injury. Leicester, Coventry and Stafford were all hit by a few bombs, while Norfolk aerodromes were again awakened more than once by the crump of bombs—either distant or nearer.

The pattern was beginning to be set now, with night raids whenever the weather permitted. And as this was midsummer, the Germans were able to take off on most nights. The variable factor was really the targets. This time on 27–28 June they turned out to be the by now familiar East Anglian and Lincolnshire aerodromes and Midland industrial areas—plus the new ingredient of the Liverpool area. Bombs were recorded right across England from Grantham to the Wirral Peninsula. At Scunthorpe, one incendiary destroyed the internal telephone exchange of the Iron Works there, but fortunately the accompanying high explosive bombs all fell on slag heaps, so caused no damage to people or property.

East Anglia took the brunt of the night's activity on 28–29 June and as well as scattered bombing, mines were probably laid off Harwich. During all this aerial action, P/O D A Williams and P/O Atkinson, his rear gunner, of 23 Squadron, repeatedly hit a Heinkel 111, making it most unlikely that the bomber ever reached its home base. On the following night, fog and rain conspired to hinder fighter action, so that no interceptions could be claimed. Less than a score of the enemy ventured over 12 Group area in darkness and among the six regions receiving the few bombs dropped were Birmingham and Stoke-on-Trent. The first mentions but not the last . . .

Night conditions cleared as June ended. Scattered bombs caused only slight damage this time, though there was a tragic outcome of the desultory raids when P/O Sisman and Sgt A Reed were killed as their Blenheim of 29 Squadron crashed near Kneeton at 01.30 hours on the night of 30 June–1 July. They were believed to have been in pursuit of an enemy bomber which was eventually brought down outside 12 Group.

Two days elapsed and then rain, low cloud and hence poor visibility all restricted fighter retaliation to raids. Ten bombs fell at Willerby; 32 incendiaries were sprayed north-east of Coventry at 01.23 hours; and seven bombs burst in the suburbs of Ipswich. Two more days and nights—and then two lone day raiders were identified in the Humber estuary and near Hull respectively.

At 00.09 hours on the night of 5–6 July, a single bomb burst near Spurn Head. Four minutes later, people heard eighteen more disturbing the same general area. Then six minutes passed—followed by a further batch of bombs south of Saltfleet. Isolated day raiders were risking the occasional hit-and-run raid and on 7 July one crossed the coast near Hapisburgh and dropped a stick of bombs near the airfield of West Rainham.

242 Squadron under Douglas Bader were fully operational both by day and night with effect from 9 July. They had a matter of mere hours to wait for their first encounters and victories. The next day, 10 July, was to mark the official start of the Battle of Britain. What more appropriate date for 242 Squadron to go into action after the impatience of their training and waiting?

Green Section, 242 Squadron, were up early that morning. While patrolling at 8,000 feet over a convoy 10 miles off Lowestoft, they sighted two Heinkel 111s. The time was 08.20 hours. P/O J B Latta spotted his first Heinkel five miles west of the convoy. Latta put on speed and was able to close with the German. His first burst, given from the stern quarter, had no effect. The next one came from astern at a range of 200 yards and enemy tracer fire soon ceased. Then he closed to 50 yards, when the enemy darted into a cloud layer at 4,000 feet, the starboard engine smoking. Latta followed through the cloud-veil but did not spot the Heinkel again. He had to presume it would be carrying on with a single engine. Whether or not it ever reached home he would probably never know. So many combats were inconclusive like that—an enemy might be shot down, but the victor would not know for sure. Latta himself received one hit on the wing of his Hurricane.

Sub Lt R E Gardner had the most decisive combat of the trio of Green Section fighters. Heading out to relieve Red Section on this convoy patrol, he first had his attention drawn to the Heinkels by AA fire from Royal Navy ships while flying at about 15,000 feet. He glimpsed a Heinkel vanish into clouds at 17,000 feet. No sooner had Gardner set his gyro on the course to encounter the enemy and climbed to 24,000 feet than he was told to return to the convoy. Back above the ships, he noticed another aircraft four miles south-east of them. Catching it up, he established it as an enemy—always an important rule to observe. He dived to the attack in direct line astern. For the second attack he came in fast at an angle of 25 degrees on the port-side. Both the port-engine and undercarriage of the enemy were hit. After a third attack, the Heinkel either crashed or pancaked into the sea at medium speed. In the two or three minutes before it sank, one of the crew climbed on to a wing . . .

The leader of the section, P/O A F Eckford, actually saw two bombs plop close to the convoy as it steamed some twelve miles south-east of Yarmouth. Eckford spotted a Heinkel 111 K Mk V A as it climbed north from 1,200 feet into the nearest available cloud cover. On emerging from the temporary shelter, the Heinkel met a long-range burst from Eckford which silenced the tracer patterning from the top gun of the bomber. Both aircraft sank into cloud and re-emerged, the Heinkel climbing south-east with a wake of white smoke. Eckford saw the other Heinkel approaching Green 2, gave chase and attacked—but lost it.

11 July 1940 meant a memorable date for Douglas Bader. It marked the morning when he shot down his very first enemy aircraft. There would be a score or so confirmed successes to come in the next year or so, but this was to be the first. Yet before this, the Germans were busy in the early hours dropping bombs in scattered districts. 85 Squadron, Yellow Section, intercepted a Dornier as it approached Yarmouth. Yellow leader, Squadron Leader Townsend made positive contact but unfortunately his fighter was hit and the Dornier escaped. Townsend had to bale out and was picked up safely—and not too seriously injured. That was the main thing.

So to Bader. Throughout the whole period from midnight to 08.30 hours on 11 July, the weather remained wretched and any interception most difficult. Flying was bad enough. Fighting virtually out of the question.

Raid 22 represented a lone Dornier 17. At dawn the report reached 12 Group that the bomber was attacking Cromer and also machine-gunning searchlights. Despite appalling visibility and with heavy rain precipitating from low clouds, Squadron Leader Bader took off at about 06.00 hours and somehow sighted the Dornier 17 a couple of miles off the Norfolk coast from Cromer. At an altitude of only 1,500 feet, Bader made two attacks. The first from 100 yards or so was head-on for two seconds, turning into a second burst of six seconds from a stern attack made at 150 yards distant. Through the rain spattering the screen, Bader saw his tracer hitting the Dornier. One brief burst from the enemy rear-gunner lit up the late-dawn gloom. Bader did not see anything more, losing sight of the enemy in a particularly dense rain cloud. After Bader returned to base he heard a report from the Royal Observer Corps at Norwich that the Dornier 17 had been actually seen to crash into the sea off Cromer at the exact time he had delivered the attack. The 12 Group log recorded that morning: 'The Battle of Britain has now started.'

It also added that the London Gazette had announced the award of the CB (Military) to Air Vice Marshal Leigh-Mallory, who would soon be giving strong support to Douglas and his views on the battle yet to develop. Sgn Ldr H W Mermagen and Sgn Ldr P C Pinkham each received the AFC.

That night of 11–12 July, seven bombs exploded near Worksop, four at Fulston, four near North Coates, and four more at Louth. Then at 08.24 hours an enemy squadron crossed the coast near Felixstowe flying at 8,000 feet. Sections of 17, 19 and 85 Squadrons went up to intercept, which they did 'in no uncertain manner.' The Germans veered off in the direction of the Convoy Booty, plodding through the North Sea, but they were quickly caught. Four Heinkel 111s and a Dornier 17 were shot down. Throughout the running engagement, the RAF lost one Hurricane and its pilot Sgt Jowett was listed as missing.

For 12 Group there followed a five-day lull in activities, partly due to weather that was poor for this time of year. Even when German raids resumed, they still seemed desultory in character. One bomber attacked some shipping off Felixstowe and also dropped a few bombs between Colchester and Braintree. Another raider circled the Humber-Hornsea region, loosing bombs near an Army post on the coast north of Hornsea at 07.12 hours. The bomber descended to a mere 100 feet and machine-gunned the post together with a cluster of bungalows occupied by troops. The soldiers valiantly but vainly tried to shoot him down with their Bren guns. It was still this sort of small-scale almost personal war, though not for much longer.

On 20 July between the times of 15.09 and 16.14 hours, 66 Squadron, Blue Section, intercepted an aircraft identified as a Blenheim. But when challenged by them, the rear gunner replied with tracer fire. They realised their error quickly, though not before the bomber had got away. It was a dirty grey tone and bore no markings. In another raid, four bombs fell east of Aylesham. And a few minutes later, just before midnight, a cluster of incendiaries lit up the Sunnyhill district of Derby.

Never at a loss for some new terror, the Germans dropped some whistling bombs on Honnington during early morning attacks. While magnetic mines laid in the Humber were promptly swept up by the Royal Navy. That was 22 July. On 23 July, heavier night bombing embraced attacks south-west of Skegness, around the Humber, north of Grimsby and south-west of the same port. Half a dozen bombs fell west of Yarmouth. On convoy patrol, Flt Lt Tawall-Sheddon used 2,400 rounds on a Junkers 86, badly damaging it, then at 16.50 hours a Dornier 215 dropped bombs near Harleston but escaped before Bader's 242 Squadron could establish contact.

A couple of days later, 222 Squadron, Red Section, met a pair of Heinkel 111s while patrolling over Convoy Pilot. P/O Vigors and P/O Assheton went for one of the Heinkels while P/O Cutts set about the other one. Both bombers were badly knocked out, and later messages received from the Air Ministry said that one of the Heinkels communicated to his home base that he could not get back. P/O Cutts ran out of fuel completely and had to make a forced-landing on the sea—no minor feat. Luckily he was picked up uninjured. Another precious pilot saved. Dowding would be grateful for that in September.

Between midnight and 04.00 hours on the night of 28–29 July, hostile raiders made their targets Loughborough, Crewe, Liverpool, Birmingham and Sealand—a distinct shift of emphasis. During daylight some 60 aircraft were plotted in 12 Group, though only Raid 10 actually dropped any bombs—six on the foreshore at Grimsby.

Shortly after lunchtime at 14.05 hours, F/O Woods-Scawen of 85 Squadron, Blue Section, was patrolling Convoy Agent when he saw and attacked a Dornier 17 about 45 miles east of Felixstowe. He opened fire at 8,000 feet altitude and chased it all the way to the Dutch coast, when he saw pieces falling from it. But then he took a quick look at his fuel gauge, made a mental calculation and swung around rapidly for home.

Exactly an hour later, 17 Squadron, Blue Section, shot down one Heinkel 111 between them. Two other Heinkels also approaching that same Convoy Agent managed to scuttle for safety. But at least they had been deterred from attempting to attack the convoy. 66 Squadron, Blue Section, accounted for another Heinkel 111 shooting it down 24 miles south-east of Lowestoft. Green Section of the same squadron were convinced that yet a third Heinkel would not stagger to its base after their concentrated fire on it.

Dawn raids seemed to be the order of these days with the Germans just at this phase. One crossed the coast north of Yarmouth and dropped 20 bombs on Norwich at 06.04 hours. That afternoon, about 15.30 hours, F/Lt Hamilton and F/Sgt Allard claimed a Messerschmitt 110 while doing their particular stint patrolling Convoy Pilot. Then a quiet day following this gave 12 Group a chance to tally up that they had sent up 1101 patrols during July, involving

2668 operational flights. Some recognition of the achievements so far were recorded by the announcement of the award of the DFC to Wg Cdr J H Edwardes-Jones, Sgn Ldr J S O'Brien and F/Lt B J E Lane—all prominent among the patrols and sorties throughout July. Although August was to be busier, it would still be frustrating for 12 Group—until the thirtieth . . .

CHAPTER 2

Fights and Frustrations

On its very first day, August was heralded with hostile raids and bombs near 12 Group airfields of Wattisham and Martlesham Heath. The enemy clearly knew their locations well by then. While patrolling Convoy Pilot from 17.47–19.20 hours, 242 Squadron were once more in action. Green Section sighted two Junkers 88s and a Heinkel 111. This is what happened next.

The personnel of pilots flying in 242 Squadron B Flight, Green Section, were F/O G P Christie (Green 1), P/O J B Latta (Green 2), and Sgt Richardson (Green 3). Christie was cruising in a climb at 200 mph about 18.10 hours when he saw the familiar form of a Junkers 88 heading east some 25 miles out of Lowestoft. The Junkers looked to be a shade of pale green underneath with dark camouflage on top. Christie was piloting his Hurricane at about 800 feet above sea-level and the bomber appeared to be a bit higher, perhaps 1,000 feet, and half a mile distant. It became aware of the Hurricane and immediately climbed steeply into cloud.

Christie was leading Green Section in open echelon. He left it and fired a brief burst from below towards the enemy starboard quarters just as the Junkers found the clouds. Christie ascended above the cover and, not finding the bomber, he told Green 2 and 3 to take over the convoy patrol while he continued the search. The Junkers broke cover three minutes later a couple of miles east of him. The same drill repeated itself: attack and then disappearance into cover. Christie could not find it again, so returned to rejoin the patrol.

At 18.25 hours he sighted another Junkers 88 just at cloud base. It sped into cover and Christie followed on the same course, but underneath the clouds. He spotted the Junkers in light cloud so pulled up and attacked it from below—while climbing almost vertically. Not the best position given a choice. But he had none. He fired a two-second full deflection shot before his Hurricane, still climbing, stalled.

Once more Christie returned to the patrol and this time a Heinkel 111 K V swept out of cloud just in front of him. The enemy rear lower gun opened up at the Hurricane as the Heinkel dropped its bombs at the convoy–but both attacks missed. The enemy was flying due west when Christie attacked, and it at once sought the clouds. Inaccurate tracer fire came from the bomber. Christie pressed home his attack as the enemy climbed into the sanctuary of cloud, and he saw a piece of starboard wing break away beside the motor. Encouraged by this evidence, Christie persevered in following him up through the cloud and took a snap shot in a small wispy gap from a range of only 50 yards. Both the starboard wing and motor were definitely damaged by then, but as Christie had little petrol left he could not continue the search for more than a few minutes.

Meanwhile Sgt Richardson sighted his Junkers 88 at 18.55 hours with the help of AA fire. Flying at some 700 feet 15 miles east of Lowestoft, the Junkers could not be mistaken, with its black crosses outlined on the side of the fuselage in white. Richardson flew into a rear quarter attack. The Junkers tried to regain cloud cover. The Hurricane broke away to the rear of the bomber and turned right. Overtaking the Junkers on its starboard side, Richardson made a front quarter attack this time, which developed into a beam one. He noticed that, even before pressing his button to fire, the enemy starboard engine had stopped. Richardson broke away to the rear, veered right again, and saw thick grey smoke trailing from the Junkers. A familiar sight in the weeks ahead.

The bomber began a very shallow though inexorable dive and when just a few feet above the waterline, its nose rose steeply so that the tail touched the sea first. The aircraft broke in two and sank within thirty seconds or so. No-one was timing exactly. Richardson circled the scene and saw a rubber boat break surface on top of the wreckage–and drift slowly away from it. Only a single survivor was seen in the water and he vanished from view soon afterwards. No-one appeared to be in the rubber boat. Richardson rejoined the rest of his section over the convoy area . . .

While Christie and Richardson were busy with their respective bombers, P/O J B Latta flying Green 2 saw a succession of enemy aircraft, which appeared over the convoy at about five-minute intervals. They sneaked out of the cloud singly and stayed exposed for no more than ten seconds at a time. Latta managed to position himself to get in two or three bursts at them. Whenever a bomber emerged from the clouds and saw that Latta or the others were a safe distance off, the Germans would let go a bomb and scuttle back into the clouds again. Latta counted four bombs released in this rather indiscriminate manner, none threateningly close to the convoy. As the Junkers and Heinkels kept coming around several times, no-one could know for sure how many they totalled, perhaps just a couple of each type. Latta could at least confirm the destruction of the Junkers 88 by Sgt Richardson. The three Hurricanes linked up and landed at 19.20 hours after an eventful patrol.

Next day several raiders approached North Sea convoys, but they faded or ran for it on finding fighters patrolling the ships. One of the Blenheims on duty unfortunately destroyed a Battle aircraft which failed to give the correct response signals—an easy mistake to make by both crews.

Small spasmodic raids characterised the next. One night an intruder came up from as far afield as South Wales, dropped four bombs near Ternhill, a further four outside Alfreton, and left 12 Group heading south. Cheeky. Another night, Crewe Junction was the target—while bombs fell harmlessly into the sea off Spurn Head too. A long hostile reconnaissance raider came across via Gloucester and Preston to Wittering and Duxford, obviously looking for 12 Group aerodromes. Three or four days later, P/O C F Cardnall and Sgt Stephens were killed when their Blenheim of 23 Squadron crashed near Peterborough while on routine patrol. Little enemy action occurred within 12 Group during that day of 8 August—in contrast to further south. A major offensive was reported in the Channel against Convoy Pewit, which sustained three attacks by more than 100 aircraft.

So it went on. The frustration of 12 Group aircrew was beginning to be felt more and more—and would continue until 30 August. On 12 August the hectic air activity in the south was marked by German onslaughts against RDF Stations, shipping in the Thames Estuary, and similar targets off the Isle of Wight, Porstmouth and Southampton. The 12 Group bombing was still on a comparatively small scale, with some damage at York, Harrogate, Leeds, Pocklington, Flint, Ilkeston and Horncastle.

On the night of 13–14 August, no contact could be recorded with the bombers, although the customary night patrols took off. Birmingham, Leamington and Wolverhampton were among the list of places visited, and although the Birmingham area received heavy bombing, no serious damage had to be admitted. Empty parachutes dropped in Derbyshire and Yorkshire turned out to be a rather feeble attempt by the Luftwaffe to cause panic among the staunch civilian population of those counties. Just another idea that misfired. Then during daylight a lone raider loosed bombs near Sealand before being identified as a Heinkel 111. A patrol ordered up to intercept this bomber was unavailable in time—so three officers from No 7 Officers Training Unit at Hawarden took off instead and actually shot down the Heinkel just north of Chester at 21.31 hours.

One of the historic days in the Battle of Britain was 15 August. 12 Group recorded 'tremendous enemy activity all around the coast of England today,' and for the first time the Germans paid a mass day visit to the group—'a day they will probably remember'. Raid 10 was initially plotted as 20+ enemy aircraft and then changed to 30+ soon afterwards. Before crossing the East Coast, it split into seven or eight separate raids. The object of the attack clarified as being Driffield aerodrome. 616 Squadron and 73 Squadron A Flight roared up to deal with the multi-pronged thrust. When finally seen, the enemy turned out to be not 20+ or 30+ but 40 Junkers 88s escorted by Messerschmitt 110s. The latter completely failed in their protective role as only a few were ever spotted by RAF pilots.

Quite a few of the bombers got through to Driffield, however, and up to 80 bombs cratered the aerodrome or its environs. If anyone on the ground had paused to take a panoramic view of the aftermath they would have witnessed three main hangars set on fire, the officers' mess badly damaged, and the anti-aircraft headquarters hit. Seven aircraft caught parked on the ground received variable damage and aerodrome personnel suffered several casualties too. The war was coming closer to everyone—aviators and ground crews. This was the first real taste of the Luftwaffe's force in the 12 Group area, but the enemy paid a substantial sum in aircraft and aircrew for the raid.

616 and 73 Squadrons claimed 15 Junkers 88s destroyed, 7 probables and 4 badly damaged. In addition perhaps half a dozen Junkers 88s were shot down or hit by ground defences. RAF fighters came out of the conflict virtually unscathed, with one aircraft hit by precisely two bullets. The individual squadron claims were as follows: 616 Squadron, 8 destroyed, 4 probables, and 2 damaged; 73 Squadron, 7 destroyed, 3 probables, and 2 damaged.

The air war was definitely moving into a higher gear. Next day, Birmingham and Coventry were prime targets with four or five other subsidiary ones. Towards evening, 19 Squadron A Flight were returning from Coltishall to Duxford when they were suddenly told over the air to intercept Raid X42 near Clacton. This modest force of one flight stumbled on some 80 Heinkel 111s with 50 Messerschmitt 110s escorting them from a greater height. The time was 17.50 hours. 'A' Flight plunged into some of the Messerschmitts and a dogfight erupted in a tracery of abstracts: pink-flecked, torn trails. Three of the Messerschmitts were claimed as shot down with another one probably destroyed.

P/O W Cunningham was one of the pilots in the little RAF band.

He opened against a particular Messerschmitt 110 with a burst astern, followed by a longer one as the enemy stall-turned—presenting its under-surface as a sitting target. Cunningham continued to fire as the enemy broke off and relapsed into a vertical dive. It fell from 12,000 feet to 2,500 feet, when it entered a cloud. Considering the speed it was descending and as the base of the cloud represented an altitude of only 1,000 feet, it would have been an aerodynamic impossibility for the Messerschmitt to have pulled out of this dive in the limited available air space. Yet Cunningham only claimed this as a probable. Another of the RAF fighters got two bullets in his port mainplane. If many pilots had not sustained trouble with gun stoppages. more of the enemy would probably have been hit.

310 Squadron (Czech) became operational at Duxford on 17 August. This was soon to become one of Bader's famous five squadrons forming the 12 Group Wing. The Czechs would be in action on their own even sooner—in just over a week. Some celebrated squadrons were now operational in 12 Group, the latest being 74 Squadron, ready at Wittering by 19 August. That same day, as well as bombing of industrial zones, a quartet of bombs landed on Broughton aerodrome. At 14.00 hours a lone bomber emerged from fleecy clouds to hit Coltishall aerodrome and cause casualties among civilian workmen. So the war was now nearer to everyone in uniform or out of it. Then at 16.15 hours other raiders made a similar hit-and-run strike at Honington, fleeing into cloud the moment their bombs were released. But 66 Squadron probably disposed of a Heinkel 111 some 30 miles east of Cromer, the enemy emitting a dark smoke trail as it faded from view, like a wounded animal.

Ten days to go now until 30 August . . . Another notable squadron joined the illustrious ranks of 12 Group. 302 Polish Squadron were ready at Leconfield, and from their very first day they were really right amid the action. But before this, the night yielded intense enemy activity. Most raiders entered the Midlands via the East Coast, and as well as hearing the live throb of their engines, the defenders saw a number of parachute flares which were dropped trying to identify either their locations or targets. Bombs fell around *23* towns—including Sheffield, Leicester, Barnsley and Warwick. Bombs aimed once more at Driffield aerodrome mangled one of the main hangars. Incendiaries cascaded on Norwich, while Derby was also hit. No military damage resulted, though some houses were hit, people killed, and both gas and water mains burst.

The only actual hostile intention during the hours of 09.00 and 13.30 on 20 August was a combined bomb and machine-gun dive on the little coastal township of Southwold. 66 Squadron A Flight all appeared to go for the same one of three Messerschmitt 110s causing this commotion, and not surprisingly with these odds it nose-dived into the North Sea four miles south of Lowestoft at precisely 10.44 hours. The day ended with the Polish 302 Squadron, Green Section, in initial combat within 12 Group. Raid X22 crossed the coast near Withernsea and made for the port of Grimsby. The Polish section comprised Sgn Ldr Satchell, P/O Wapniarek and F/Lt Jastrebski. They traced the raider, a Junkers 88, and riddled it three times over. It crashed into the sea at around 19.10 hours. One less of the Luftwaffe.

An occasion to remember was the first time that these squadrons of what would shortly become the Bader Wing flew on the same day—21 August. Not yet as a wing but separated by only an hour or two. Already there seemed a certain inevitability about the way events were moving. One of these squadrons was the Polish 302. Another was 611 Squadron of Spitfires. The third, of course, 242 Squadron.

The day started in typical fashion for August. At 08.00 hours a raider slipped across the coastline and dropped five bombs on Bircham Newton—demolishing the married quarters there. The bomber merged into the moving clouds as quickly as it had come. Also at breakfast time, another raider did the same sort of thing at Stradishall aerodrome. This kind of nuisance activity continued on and off all day, but in the air RAF fighters scored successes: four enemy shot down. The main enemy objectives were aerodromes and shipping, with the raids aided by broken clouds typical of the month's weather.

242 Squadron was the first of the trio in action. B Flight, Blue Section, were ordered to patrol the Norwich region at noon. The section flew as F/Lt G S Powell-Sheddon (Blue 1), P/O Latta (Blue 2) and S/Lt R E Gardner (Blue 3). Ten minutes after the call came to scramble, the section found themselves over the cathedral city. First given a vector of 190°, they then rapidly received an amendment to 240°. At a split-second timing between 12.14 and 12.15 hours they all saw a Dornier 17 cruising at about 200 mph on a course of 270° magnetic. The sighting occurred 20 miles south of Norwich while the enemy bomber was at only 3,500 feet and sandwiched between two layers of broken cloud.

The moment they spotted the bomber, it dived for the lower layer of cumulus. As the Dornier veered left and downward into the bank, Powell-Sheddon took a single-second deflection shot at it. Following through the cover, Blue 1 saw the bomber beyond, still turning to port and diving slightly. Blue 1 spurted to a position just over 100 yards away from the aircraft and spat another burst from beam astern. Two seconds this time. Blue 1 saw no effect from these bursts and in fact the Dornier retaliated by opening up all its guns on him. Cannon plus two machine-guns from the rear and underneath. Tracer bullets etched through the cloud mask. So strong was the counter-attack that Blue 1 had to break off to the right.

Following hard on the trail of Blue 1, Blue 2 found himself 100 yards from the Dornier and underneath, so fired a six-second stream from below with a deflection of 25°. Meanwhile Blue 3 also emerged from the 8/10ths intermittent cloud to find Blue 1 attacking, so he could not open fire at that stage. There was always that danger of hitting one's own side. Then he saw a free moment and concentrated on the enemy port engine from 250 yards. It lit up like a gas jet in a strong draught. Then Blue 3 transferred his fire to the fuselage which also showed flame signs after seven or eight seconds. Blue 3 closed to . . . 20 yards. Oil from the Dornier clung to his fighter.

Blue 1 was thwarted from making a third attack on the starboard beam due to Blue 3's presence. By then all three Hurricane pilots could see smoke and flames, while no further firing came from the spiralling bomber. The Dornier was failing and falling. Two of the crew baled out but the pilot stuck to his aircraft, flying perilously low over a village eight miles west of Harleston. It staggered on as the pilot tried to pancake in a field on the far side of the village. But he could not control the crippled Dornier and overshot the field. The bomber bounced into a small wood beyond the field and dissolved into a familiar mixture of smoke and flame. The fire consumed the black crosses and little was left of it. Powell-Sheddon landed with the other two at 12.37 hours to find he had a torn tailplane and a dent in the tailplane span. These were caused not by firing from the bomber but by fragments flying off it at close range —always an additional hazard to fighters. The destruction of the Dornier was credited jointly to all three of Blue Section. This sort of experience was invaluable for them in preparing for the days ahead.

Douglas Bader got his eye in within an hour of this patrol. Various R/T messages intercepted made him realise that there were enemy bombers in the vicinity, so although he had been detailed only for 'local flying' and was not ordered off, he rolled his Hurricane at 13.00 hours and took it up to 9,000 feet. Quarter of an hour later he was three miles north-west of Yarmouth and making a head-on quarter attack on a Dornier 17 from 250 yards, turning into a straight attack at 200 yards. He got in a couple of six-second bursts as the Dornier scurried for cloud. He saw his tracer striking the enemy, but nothing more definite than that.

The Dornier was coloured duck-egg blue underneath with black on top. It flew roughly ESE at 180–200 mph and its tactics consisted of a straight shallow dive for cloud cover. As Douglas fired at the Dornier it was only about 100 feet above cloud, so things happened hurriedly. The enemy rear-gunner fired a machine-gun from above the fuselage—and weights attached to long wire were thrown out from under the fuselage. As Bader was almost on the same level as the bomber, these passed underneath him causing no inconvenience or damage to his Hurricane.

Before the Dornier disappeared the rear-gunner only got in a single short sally at him then appeared to have been hit—as he stopped soon after Bader started firing his first burst from astern. A lone bullet struck the fighter, in the middle of the leading edge of the port wing. So ended a rather inconclusive exchange, but Bader would soon be in more serious and large-scale action.

As 242 Squadron landed at 12.37 hours, 611 Squadron were in another scrap. Red Section consisted of F/O D H Watkins, P/O M P Brown and P/O J W Lund. They accounted for a Dornier 215 and probably a second one, four miles east of 'bracing' Skegness. At 12.38 hours, a minute after 242 Squadron landed, 611 Squadron A Flight, Red Section, spotted three Dornier 215s. P/O Brown was flying as Red 2 at 4,500 feet when he went for the Dorniers with his leader in echelon port. Brown and Red 3 took the number three bomber and soon saw both engines fuming. Brown's fire entered the Dornier—he could vouch for that visibly. After breaking off the burst, he saw one of the bombers vortex towards the North Sea with two of the crew baling out frantically. Would they survive the water even if they reached it alive? But before the bomber finally sent up a spume of seawater, other enemy bullets had penetrated Brown's port and starboard wings, burst one of his tyres, and ripped through his rudder. Somehow he hobbled back to base to discover all this damage.

The Yellow Section 611 Squadron—Sgn/Ldr J E McComb, Sgt A D Burt and Sgt A S Darling—intercepted a quartet of Dorniers after they had dropped a score or more bombs on the naval shore establishment of HMS Royal Arthur at Skegness. Then after a brief encounter with a Dornier 215, which fizzed frightened into the clouds, they ran slap into a trio of Dornier 17s. This V formation arrived into view at 13.14 hours, heading inland. Yellow 2 returned tracer from the first bomber, whereupon enemy fire ceased from that source. But Yellow 2 became badly caught in the enemy's slipstream as the Spitfire followed up its thrust rather enthusiastically. He managed to pull up his nose with a jerk and fire again. After losing the Dornier momentarily, he opened his throttle and nearly rammed the enemy right in the thick of the clouds. He pulled away violently to port to avoid any collision. A plume of smoke waved from the starboard engine of the Dornier. The outcome of this action with Yellow 1, 2 and 3 was that two Dornier 17s were shot down near Skegness. Seven aircrew baled out of these two machines and were taken prisoner on touching the ground. So they were the lucky ones . . .

The third of the trio of squadrons in action was 302 Polish, Blue Section. Flying as Blue 2, P/O Calupa was patrolling over the sea at 12,000 feet when the silhouette of a Junkers 88 manifested itself on the port side. The time registered 15.50 hours as Blue 1 turned to attack from above and behind. Three bursts caused fragments to fly off the Junkers before it made for cloud, pursued passionately by the trio of Blue Section. Neither Blue 1 nor Blue 2 caught sight of it again after the bomber successfully sought cover.

Their next engagement proved to be more spectacular. Blue 2 spotted an enemy aircraft half a mile off. Chalupa approached his section leader, waggled his wings to draw attention to the raider, and then veered off in that direction. As Chalupa was flying into the sun, he could not really recognise the enemy at once. Then with the sun slightly on his starboard bow, at 200 yards he identified it as a Junkers 88.

Three bursts later from 150 yards and he saw 'certain objects' flying from the Junkers, and smoke permeating its port engine area. It started to dive for clouds. At this moment, Chalupa's engine began to cough badly and emit whitish smoke from beneath the cowling. The encounter had happened two miles east of Bridlington. Now the Polish pilot had to throttle back and try to glide towards his home aerodrome. The altitude was dropping below the 2,000 feet mark when the engine really started to vibrate, as if shuddering with a fever. Chalupa persevered. He did not drop his undercarriage, nor was he able quite to reach the runway. Nevertheless, the Hurricane lurched down towards the edge of the aerodrome, where the Pole managed to put it on terra firma without any serious injury either to himself or his precious aircraft. The Junkers crashed and was credited to 302 Squadron.

Enemy raids on Wansford, Allwalton, Sheringham and Southwold rounded off the day: a date giving Bader and his pilots a tantalising taste of what would be possible given the circumstances and opportunity. They were beginning to become impatient for larger-scale action: the sort of scraps that 11 Group were already fighting. But that night and next morning strong winds and rain in all areas curtailed flying almost entirely. Typically British summer weather, one Canadian cynic said. Bader and the rest had another full week to wait before the combats they were all wishing for so strenuously.

In the early hours of 23 August, magnetic mines were laid in the Humber; Raid 47 dropped bombs near Warrington; Raid 38 bombed and machine-gunned the front-line town of Bridlington, at times flying a mere 50 feet over the boarding houses of that normally peaceful resort: and another half dozen towns were hit. In the three hours before noon, a dozen hostile raids neared Norfolk, but none crossed the coastline. Misty weather may have been the reason. It certainly meant that none of our fighters could manage to make contact with the enemy. The Duxford ground guns claimed a Dornier 17 nearby at Wickhambrook to alleviate yet another frustrating day.

On the next night, air activity switched to the industrial areas around Birmingham. Bombs were recorded in the city itself, Kidderminster and King's Lynn. One of them could have been the bomb rendered safe in King's Lynn years later by Major Bill Hartley, as head of Bomb Disposal. At 07.45 hours a raider crossed the coast near Winterton and dropped 20 bombs on the unsuspecting town of Gorleston, also hitting it with machine-gun fire.

During that afternoon, 12 Group had its aggressive appetite whetted when 19, 310 and 66 Squadrons were despatched to assist 11 Group. They caught up with the Luftwaffe over the mouth of the Thames—a considerable force of both bombers and fighters. But the conditions were not conducive to catching the enemy and only 19 Squadron actually met them.

Sgt B J Jennings got near enough to a Messerschmitt 110 to fire. He hit the starboard engine and propeller—the latter falling off and dragging parts of the engine along too. Jennings could not follow down, due to the overtaking speed and his having to tackle other fighters. But the Messerschmitt went into a vicious engine turn and steep dive to starboard. It was only classed as a probable victory, though its erratic behaviour suggested it must become a total loss.

Jennings then galloped after another one. After firing a fairly long burst, he witnessed the rather unearthly spectacle of the starboard rudder, tail fin and a major chunk of tailplane, all floating and falling—almost as if weightless for an instant. The Messerschmitt 110 swung and dived to port, anguished in its death throes. Jennings did not actually stay to see it crash, as two more of the same type arrived on his immediate air-scene. He survived the day. Pilots were beginning to learn that this was as much as they could expect . . .

Maximum activity, minimum bombs, this summarised the night raids which seemed to be principally reconnaissance. But scattered bombs caused nuisance value at no fewer than nineteen places in the area. Leeds was on the list now too. Twenty-one places on the next night. And though no aerodromes had direct hits, bombs exploded audibly nearby.

During the day of 26 August, four squadrons of 12 Group went to help 11 Group combat a raid over the Thames Estuary. They were 310, 66, 19 and 229 Squadrons, but only 310 contacted the enemy. Sgn Ldr G D Blackwood was leading 310 Squadron at 15.35 hours near North Weald when his dozen aircraft saw as many or more Dornier 215s. As Blackwood had the only fighter fitted with VHF radio, he could not give any orders for a particular type of attack. So he just dived in from astern and hopefully opened up at 600 yards closing. He had no alternative but to back away when intense fire from the rear of the formation scorched around him.

Still at some 12,000 feet, he noticed a Dornier slightly apart from the rest, so for his next onslaught he chose this one. The range had halved to 300 yards and his astern attack seemed to catch the bomber unawares. It wobbled perceptibly, apparently either trying to take some evasive cause or else being out of control.

But Blackwood suddenly smelt something burning. He looked around rapidly in the confined cockpit, to see his starboard wing-tank blistering on the top side of the wing. He decided instantly to break off the attack and concentrate instead on survival. He then realised that his petrol tank was burning inside. About ten seconds later, the tank flared into flames, so Blackwood undid his straps urgently and disconnected his oxygen tube. Following the prescribed drill meticulously, calmly, quickly, he turned over the aircraft on its back and he simply fell out. Blackwood wafted down safely, landing in a stubble field with no personal damage. One aircraft lost. One pilot saved.

Sgt Prohal delivered his first attack with his squadron leader and then broke off when he saw the Dornier diving enveloped in fire, out of control, and followed by other Hurricanes. Prohal tried to tackle the rest of the formation, diving in from astern. But really intensified fire forced him to break. A third effort from starboard and sun did not seem successful either, so he tried it again–firing from 400 down to 60 yards. The target aircraft spurted flames from the port engine as it limped into the clouds.

Prohal climbed above the clouds and moved into another phase of his own personal battle. He headed for a group of Messerschmitt 109s and fired fruitlessly. As he lost touch with them, he set course for the coast in the Clacton/Southend region. Over to the left he saw what he thought was a Spitfire, owing to its wing configuration. But on coming closer he had the jolt of realising it was actually a Heinkel 112. Prohal regained a level position at 5,000 feet to prepare an attack, but as he did so another enemy machine aimed a short snap of cannon and gun fire at him. Bullets from the machine-guns literally tore into his Glycol tank, port wing and rudders. Prohal instinctively made a steep starboard turn. His cockpit became choked with vapour from the glycol. He could not see the compasss, so he flew by the sun with the object of landing as soon as he saw the coast. By gliding from the altitude of the clouds, he came down to land level with his undercarriage up and 3½ miles south-east of Hornchurch in Essex. The fighter made a forced landing. Prohal was slightly wounded he found out afterwards, with splinters penetrating his shoulders, left arm and neck. But he was alive.

Blackwood and Prohal had been in Flight A of 310 Squadron. P/O Emil Fechtner was Flight B, Green Section. After they had all launched their offensive against the dozen-or-more Dorniers, Fechtner followed a Messerschmitt 110, aiming a substantial burst of 1200 rounds at him as the range shortened from 250 to 100 yards. The usual heavy black smoke from one of the enemy's engines left a trail from 15,000 feet downward. Fechtner was ready to finish off the adversary, but suddenly six Messerschmitt 109s flying in Vic formation zoomed at him. He wisely found refuge in the clouds and set course for base. His action had been over the Harwich environs. Now no boats left that port for the Continent. Fechtner flew fast for 4 minutes, crossing both the railway line and the road leading to Chelmsford and Colchester. Prudence had ensured his survival.

Night raids were repeated on the Midland industrial targets and widespread aerodromes. The bombers came into 12 Group from both the south corridor and the east. Birmingham suffered a long and damaging raid. People were killed. Eighteen other places too. Between one and two hundred incendiaries rained on North Coates aerodrome but with little fire damage. Nor did the fires started in Birmingham spread too much.

12 Group had to wait only a couple of days more for action on a heroic scale. Meanwhile, the group had its heaviest night raids to date on 27–28 August. Both Birmingham and Yorkshire industry had hits, while the Humber docks received their share. Raiders actually entered 12 Group zone from all directions except the west. Fire broke out near the Nuffield factory at Birmingham, and two delayed action weapons fell in Section C of the same works. When they eventually went off, they did only minimal damage due to the precautions taken. The strategy was successfully tried of blacking out Birmingham and Norwich as far as searchlights were concerned. This did in fact seem to make it harder for the bombers to locate their targets with any accuracy. Twenty-seven places were bombed. One 500-pounder dropped on the previous night exploded on

Kirton-in-Lindsey aerodrome. Danger to a hangar and a runway resulted, but fortunately not to any personnel. An enemy seaplane landed on the water off Mablethorpe and remained there for some measurable time!

The next night raids on 28–29 August spanned six hours or more, from 21.20 to 03.30 hours. The worst hit areas were Derby, Sheffield, Manchester, Barnsley, Leeds and Liverpool. Derby suffered a special volume of bombs, but Coventry and Birmingham enjoyed a quiet night for a change. But spare a second to read the list of targets that night, spread as far apart as Bircham Newton, West Raynham, Aylsham, Finningley, Horncastle, Melton Mowbray, Grantham, Digby, Mablethorpe, Daventry, Brackley, Spalding, Manchester, Goole, Grimsby, Warrington, Skipton, Louth, Crewe, Rochdale, Stenigot, Sealand, Northwich, Barnsley, Leeds, Liverpool, Sheffield, Huddersfield, Chester and Derby. Quite a list. 12 Group read about it next day with mounting impatience . . .

Shot down somewhere in England, 18 August 1940: the partly burnt wreck of a Dornier viewed from the starboard front.

Formidable trio showing unofficial emblem: left to right, Flt Lt G E Ball DFC, Sqn Ldr Douglas Bader DSO, and P/O Willie McKnight DFC. The place and time: Duxford, September 1940.

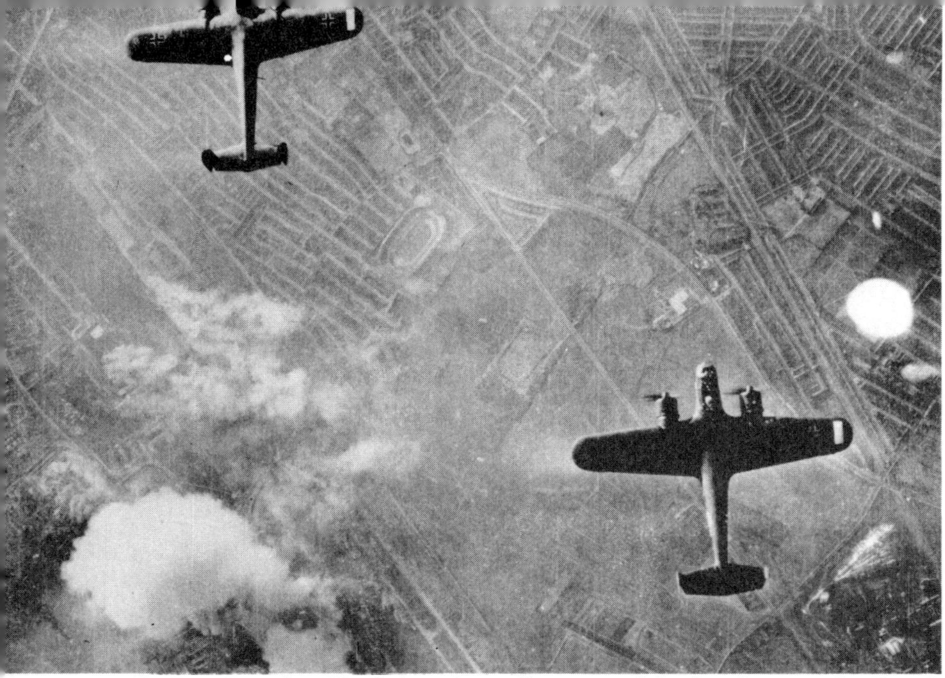

3. Two Dornier 17s flying above fires started by bombs near the Royal Victoria Docks and West Ham areas of London. 7 September 1940.

4. On 15 September 1940, Flt Lt Percival Stanley ("Stan") Turner succeeded in shooting down an enemy aircraft when his own aircraft was hit by a cannon shell which put it temporarily out of control. On recovery, he saw and attacked a further enemy aircraft which he destroyed, bring his own damaged aircraft safely back to its base. This officer has personally destroyed a total of ten hostile aircraft during engagements over Dunkirk and England.

CHAPTER 3

One Hundred Enemy Aircraft

Here at long last was the first of many memorable days for Douglas Bader and 242 Squadron. Friday 30 August. But before it dawned, the operations of the night were divided into two parts. The first began at 22.40 hours and was directed against west and north-west Midland industry. The second phase from 02.00 hours concentrated on the East Coast. Lancashire industrial conurbations suffered during the first period—Liverpool, Warrington and Manchester. The Observer Corps were actually unable to plot raids for some time due to the holocaust around Warrington . . .

Throughout August, Douglas and the other pilots of 12 Group became more and more impatient to get at the enemy, but they were always being held in reserve. They heard the growing number of reports on the gathering momentum of mass attacks in the South—and ached to join in the affray. Earlier on, Douglas had been flying Spitfires and he could get in and out of his machine more quickly with his artificial legs than most other pilots with their real ones. He had already been in action several times and once when taking off, his engine had failed and he suffered a mild crash. The result was that both Bader's metal legs became bent, but an artificer straightened them and half an hour later he was up in the air again.

But now he was flying Hurricanes, and it was the sort of war where a German flyer fired at a Hurricane pilot parachuting down from a wrecked fighter—and killed him.

On Friday 30 August, Douglas at last led his Hurricane into action in some force. '242 Squadron scramble—Angels fifteen. North Weald.' They were off. At 16.26 hours 242 Squadron were ordered from Duxford to patrol North Weald at 15,000 feet on vector 190°. Just north of North Weald they received vector 340° Just about then, Douglas Bader's piercing eyes noticed three unidentified aeroplanes below and to the right of the squadron.

'Bandits to west. Blue Section investigate.'

So the squadron was depleted of three Hurricanes and had ten remaining. Green leader drew Bader's attention to a large Luftwaffe formation on their left. He turned with the other nine aircraft to witness what was undeniably an awe-inspiring sight—particularly to any of them who had not previously been in action. There were a vast number of twin-engined aeroplanes in front now, flying in an easterly direction. Bader counted fourteen blocks of six aircraft—all bombers—with thirty Messerschmitt 110 fighters behind and above. So altogether 242 Squadron's ten Hurricanes had more than 100 enemy aircraft to tackle. Odds of ten to one. The bombers, Heinkel 111s with perhaps some Dornier 17s as well, flew in tight formation stepped up from about 12,000 feet. Then came a gap of a thousand feet, with a swarm of fighters ranged from some 15,000–20,000 feet.

Bader could not see any friendly fighters near, so he ordered Green Section to attack the top of the lower formation of fighters, while his flight of Red and Yellow Sections went into line astern to go for the bombers. Immediately Bader had detailed F/O Christie to take his section of three to keep the Messerschmitt's busy, this pilot from Calgary said, 'O.K., O.K.' with obvious relish, and away he streaked to deal with that vastly superior number of enemy fighters.

There was obviously no point in trying to deliver any formation attack and Bader's only object was to break up the formation and start a dogfight. The enemy bombers were flying at around 15,000 feet now, with the middle of the formation roughly west of the reservoirs at Enfield and heading east. When first sighted they looked just like a vast swarm of bees. With the sun at their backs and the advantage of greater height, conditions were ideal for a surprise attack and as soon as 242 were all in position they went straight down to the Germans. Bader did not adopt any set rules in attacking—he just worked on the axiom that the shortest distance between two points is a straight line.

So he dived straight into the middle of the tightly-packed formation, closely followed by the rest of his flight—Red 2 was P/O Willie McKnight and Red 3 P/O Denis Crowley-Milling. The enemy immediately broke up fanwise. He saw three Messerschmitt 110s do climbing turns left and three to the right. Bader spotted McKnight veer left while he attacked the right-hand trio. Their tactics appeared to be climbing turns to a nearly stalled position to try to get on Bader's tail. He tried a short burst of nearly three seconds into the first Messerschmitt 110 at nearly point blank range as he was at the top of his zoom. The aeroplane seemed to burst into flames and disintegrate.

Simultaneously, Willie McKnight went for a section of Messerschmitt 110s and two enemy aircraft broke off specifically to attack him. He succeeded in getting behind one of them and opened fire at 100 yards. He hit it and it spun towards the Essex earth. He at once went for a Heinkel 111 group, executing a neat beam attack on the one nearest to him. Its port engine paused and then stopped. A second or so later the bomber rolled over on its back as if wounded and finally started to smoke. Then it conflagrated and crashed.

Meanwhile Douglas Bader continued his zoom and found a second Messerschmitt below and to his right, just starting to dive after a stalled turn. So he turned in behind the German and got a very early shot at about 100–150 yards' range. Bader's first burst lasted two to four seconds. After this, the enemy's evasive action consisted in pushing his stick violently backwards and forwards. The second time he did this manoeuvre, Douglas got in a burst as he was at the top of his short zoom. He saw pieces fly off the enemy's starboard wing near the engine and then the whole of the starboard wing went on fire. The aeroplane fell away to the right in a steep sort of spiral dive, well on fire. Bader did not see anyone bale out of either of the Messerschmitt 110s, although it is possible that they did so. He was too busy looking around to worry once they had caught fire. There just was not time to stop and think of consequences.

Bader noticed in his mirror a Messerschmitt 110 coming up behind him and he did a quick turn—to see five or six white streams coming out of the German's firing guns. It seemed as though the pilot were using tracer in all his guns. As soon as Bader turned, the Messerschmitt 110 put its nose down and Douglas temporarily lost him. Evenutally Douglas saw him travelling east far below. Bader tried to catch him but he could not, so fired no more. Not once did a Messerschmitt 110 get sights on Bader's Hurricane. Douglas saw nothing except Messerschmitt 110s, though there were Heinkels and Dorniers in force as well.

One of those Messerschmitt 110s was attacking Willie McKnight just about then, but the young Canadian pilot succeeded in getting behind. He followed the Messerschmitt 110 from 10,000 feet right down to 1,000 feet. The enemy used ultra steep turns to try and get clear, but eventually it had to straighten out or crash. McKnight opened fire at a range of 30 yards—just over the length of a cricket pitch in the sky. The enemy's starboard engine stopped; the port one flamed. It crashed after having used a lot of rear fire at McKnight. He saw it go down alongside a large reservoir.

After Bader and McKnight had gone for the Messerschmitt 110s broken off from the middle section originally, Denis Crowley-Milling flying Red 3 was left with a Heinkel 111 K open to himself. He attacked astern, giving the bomber a five-second thrust. Tentative return rear fire soon stopped as the aircraft began an inexorable descent to earth. Crowley-Milling started to follow it, when tracer bullets from a Messerschmitt 110 passed his starboard wing. He at once decided to nose away to port and in so doing lost sight of both the attacker and the Heinkel 111 K. P/O Hart confirmed that the Heinkel went down in flames.

Flt Lt G E Ball led Yellow Section as Bader's own section broke up the enemy masses. He saw a single Heinkel 111 circling, diving and turning, all at once. Ball took it from behind. He closed to 100 yards, using one-third of his ammunition. Both enemy engines caught alight and the bomber force-landed on an aerodrome full of cars near North Weald. Ball then chased a straggler Messerschmitt 110, which he finished off with a stern attack. The enemy engine stopped dead and the aircraft lost height rapidly. Ball had the sun behind him during both these attacks.

At 17.05 hours Sub Lt R J Cork RN was flying as Yellow 2 between North Weald and Hatfield when he attacked a Messerschmitt 110 in company with several other fighters. He saw the Messerschmitt going down as he broke away left after another east flying 110. Cork's beam atack hit its mark and the enemy executed a frantic stall turn with the port engine afire. There was no hope left for it as it reached the point of no return and seconds later exploded on the ground. Cork swung back to the scene of combat with both these Messerschmitt 110s and saw the first of them burning in a field. Its swastikas still stood out against the dark green body. He could claim one of the enemy as destroyed personally while the other counted as a probable. Six bursts of three seconds each had accounted for this damage.

Sgt R V Lonsdale flying as Yellow 3 sought a Heinkel 111 which had become parted from its formation. He pressed the button to start a prolonged 10-second burst beginning 300 yards away and ending only 50 yards from the Heinkel. The enemy circled like a wounded bird from this quarter attack and eventually crashed in the same area as the Messerschmitt 110 attributed to Cork. A Hurricane could and did easily outfly and outrace an opponent like a Heinkel travelling at 200 mph.

When Bader told Green Section to go for the top of the lower formation, F/O Christie as Green Leader launched a bull-like head-on charge for a Messerschmitt 110 on the top of four layers. It arced off to starboard, diving as it went. Christie kept glued to its tail, spraying a burst from 50 yards astern. Something had to hit shortly and oil started spouting, gushing, from the starboard motor. The petrol tanks burst, the Messerschmitt 110 took a vertical dive, and it travelled from 6,000 feet straight down into greenhouses about 500 yards from the reservoir at Ponder's End.

Green Section were flying behind Yellow Section when 242 Squadron saw the enemy originally. They received the orders to attack the fighters above them, but these quickly dispersed—things happened in seconds or even semi-seconds. So Green Section chose the bombers instead. Green 3, P/O N Hart, stumbled on three in line astern about 1,000 feet below his Hurricane. As he started to dive he saw Yellow 1 attacking the last one of the trio. Hart took the second bomber and sent it into a steep dive. He was just about to follow it down when the first Heinkel made a steep right-hand turn. Hart turned inside it and used up all his ammunition on the bomber. It plunged into a field with all the crew still aboard. Hart did not dwell there, as three Messerschmitt 110s began to chase him.

P/O Stansfield also attacked an enemy aircraft with Flt Lt Ball. Stansfield first saw the straggler aiming eastward. In the first of three attacks he silenced the rear gunner, who had opened fire at him with cannon. Both enemy engines were in trouble: smoke from the port, while the starboard stopped altogether. The Heinkel 111 came down heavily on a civil aerodrome covered with wrecked cars, but three Germans staggered out of its wrecked remnants. Stansfield was Black 1 and Sgt G W Brimble Black 2.

Brimble followed Stansfield on to the Heinkel, firing from 250 yards. He saw Stansfield follow the bomber almost into the ground. Then Brimble broke away to find a Messerschmitt 110 executing a gentle turn to port. He achieved a quarter attack from the same range as his previous one and had the definite sight of the enemy actually striking the ground.

As Brimble flew across to rejoin his section leader, the next thing he knew was a Messerschmitt 110 aiming straight for him. He opened fire instinctively at 350 yards and saw all the glass splinter in front of the enemy aircraft. The machine took on a violent convulsive dive, as if in some fatal fever. Brimble did not see it crash as a Messerschmitt 110 got on his tail. The rule was survival first.

Back to Bader and his advice about enemy aircraft on the tail of Hurricanes. As Douglas climbed back to 12,000 feet from 6,000, he could see no further enemy. He thought: Now, there's one curious thing about this air fighting. One minute you see hundreds of aeroplanes in the sky, and the next minute there's nothing. All you can do is to look through your sights at your particular target—and look in your mirror, too, if you are sensible, for any Messerschmitts which might be trying to get on to your tail.

Well, that particular battle lasted about five or ten minutes, and then, quite suddenly, the sky was clear of aircraft.

One pilot had sent a Hun bomber crashing into a greenhouse. Another bomber had gone headlong into a field filled with derelict motor-cars; it hit one of the cars, turned over, and caught fire. Another of 242 Squadron had seen a twin-engined job of sorts go into a reservoir near Enfield. Yet another pilot saw his victim go down with his engine flat out; the plane dived into a field and disintegrated into little pieces. Incidentally, that particular pilot brought down three Huns on this day.

242 Squadron had not shot them all down, of course. They hadn't waited for that, but made off home in all directions at high speed. But, apart from the bag of twelve, (eight Messerschmitt fighter-bombers, three Heinkel 111 bombers, and a fourth Heinkel bomber already partly damaged by another squadron), there were a number of others which were badly shot up and probably never got home—like one which went staggering out over Southend with one engine out of action.

As Douglas could spot no enemy despite his peeled eyes, he called Duxford by radio and was told to land. On the way he picked up Green Leader, F/O Christie, and also Blue Section. The infuriated Blue Section pilots had been sent off to investigate unidentified aircraft and missed the entire battle. They had not fired a single round between them and their language when they heard what they'd missed was unprintable!

One thing Douglas particularly noticed with surprise was that he received no rear gun fire from the Messerschmitt 110s and they appeared to be trying to fight with front guns only. This made the odds heavily in the Hurricane's favour, and not once did Messerschmitt 110s get sights on Bader. Which was just as well because he admitted, he saw nothing in this dog fight except his own little personal battle.

So ten Hurricanes had fought and routed over a hundred of the enemy at odds of ten to one. Such was Douglas's inspiring leadership and strategic skill.

As a result of this successful engagement the notion of a larger formation than a squadron of twelve or thirteen fighters was conceived in the mind of Air Vice Marshal Leigh-Mallory. On this particular occasion the squadron was called off the ground in time to meet a large enemy formation under favourable conditions south-west of Epping. They had position, height and sun in attacking an enemy bomber formation without Messerschmitt 109 escort. In the course of a congratulatory call from Mallory that same evening, Douglas said to him: 'If I'd had more fighters, we would have shot down more of the enemy.'

A few days later the Duxford Wing of three squadrons was actually born.

CHAPTER 4

The Bader Wing is Born

Night fell and the raids began again on industrial areas and East Anglian aerodromes. Watnall airfield was bombed for the first time, four delayed-action bombs being dropped a quarter of a mile from the camp. Two civilians were killed. Lancashire and the Mersey suffered badly, with Liverpool and Manchester worst hit. As well as these great metropolitan targets, about a dozen other areas were struck: Norwich, Digby, Cranwell, Stoke, Grantham, Derby, Peterborough, Nottingham, Wolverhampton, Skegness and Sheffield. In more than one case, a certain amount of suspected Fifth Column activity was reported, as flares had been seen to be sent up from the ground while enemy bombers were overhead or in the locality. Bulwell was one of the offending districts, only a couple of miles from Watnall, 12 Group Headquarters. Derby searchlights were switched on without orders at 22.15–23.00 hours and were promptly bombed, proving the value of the dousing strategy. Elsewhere there was good searchlight co-operation with RAF fighters along a belt roughly from Scampton–Honington.

11 Group got a surfeit of enemy activity between 08.00–09.30 hours on 31 August and Squadrons 19, 66, 229, 242, 310 and 611 were told to try and help from 12 Group. 10 Squadron was the only one to make any contact and probably hit a Messerschmitt 110. But in so doing they lost three fighters and P/O Aberhart was killed. F/O Coward was injured and F/O Brinsden baled out safely.

Just after lunch 310 Squadron of twelve aircraft took off from Duxford with orders to patrol Hornchurch at 10,000 feet. Take-off time was almost exactly 13.00 hours and North Weald also came within their patrol instructions. It had been arranged that in the event of interception both A and B flights would attack in section line astern, one from either beam and slightly above. The dive was to be continued past the enemy formation, when they would turn to port or starboard, climb and repeat the manoeuvre.

At 13.15 the squadron sighted 15 Dornier 15s in very tight grouping flying northward at some 220 mph. They had the protection of 10–20 Messerschmitt 109s, milling above and below busily. The pre-arranged tactics were pursued. Flt Lt Sinclair was leading the squadron when the Dorniers took shape, pinpointed by the bursts of anti-aircraft fire from the ground. The Germans also saw 310 Squadron simultaneously.

As they turned east, Sinclair climbed 2,000 feet and told B Flight to fly to port of the enemy while he led A Flight to the starboard. A Flight formed line astern to attack from the quarter. Sinclair picked on one at the van of the formation. He made four thrusts on the Dornier, the first two with his section behind him and the other two solo. Enemy fire ceased after attack number three and on the fourth it went into a dive. This did not stop until the Dornier met the mouth of the Thames, visibly but noiselessly. Three Messerschmitt 109s swooped on Sinclair so he dived away from that particular hostile environment.

Sqn Ldr A Hess put the engagement time at 13.25. After the first effort by A Flight, several Messerschmitts turned on Hess. He saw one of them firing at him, so he turned sharp right and climbed. A Messerschmitt 109 overshot him and he took the German from below. He hit it and the Messerschmitt spun madly out of control. Hess had to break off following it down as a pair more Messerschmitt 109s appeared. The enemy fire peppered from above but missed him. He then counter-attacked them, together with other Hurricanes of 310 Squadron. Hess spotted a Dornier 215 on the left outskirts of the group, already breaking up before his stare. He gave it a further 4–5 seconds' burst from the rear and the enemy dipped steeply. At 1,000 feet it straightened out and Hess pumped the balance of his ammunition from the rear and side. The bomber went down near the River Roach. Three of the crew jumped out and put up their hands. They had had enough of the Battle of Britain. A second Hurricane appeared and circled to see the end of that particular episode.

Ten miles north-east of London, P/O Z M Maly, also of A Flight, was set on by fighters from the rear and out of the sun. Turning left he met the unhappy sight of three Messerschmitt 109s just a hundred yards behind him. Two of them opened fire. Somehow he escaped their clutch, turned, and saw a further Messerschmitt 109 from the rear, hit it and watched it plummet. Six fighters suddenly materialised from the rear, but fortuitously they turned out to be Hurricanes! He did not actually see the Messerschmitt 109 go down, but a few seconds later Maly glimpsed a parachute four or five miles off to the north-east. He did not know whose.

Flt Lt J Jeffries was leading B Flight. The enemy hove into view about 1,000 feet above B Flight, at the 11,000 feet mark. He positioned the flight in line astern 1,000 feet above and on the port side —level with the leading aircraft of the second group. They went in from the sides and above. After the second foray, a Dornier 215 broke away apparently hit. Jeffries got in a short deflection shot at some oncoming Messerschmitt 109s, then he could do nothing much more. The Dornier 215 could be claimed as destroyed, since it was last seen ominously near ground level.

The Hurricanes sustained little or no damage during the first part of this flight, the planned tactics proving successful. But later on, the squadron became more dispersed and enemy rear gunners began to inflict some losses. All this was going on over a period of perhaps ten minutes, no more. The one major casualty was P/O Sterbacek, whose Hurricane went down in the thick of things. P/O Kredba baled out of a similarly serious situation and landed more or less intact.

P/O Emil Fechtner was leading Green Section, B Flight when his fire found engine and cockpit of a Dornier 215. Part of the cockpit snapped away. The aircraft dived on its port wing towards earth. Fechtner regained a level position and level head above the enemy group to get away safely. Just about that minute his Hurricane got hits in both wings and the tyre of the left wheel. He could not repeat his attack so made for home, landing securely at 14.00 hours.

Blue Section, B Flight dived in out of the sun, almost straight from the rear. The section all fired and registered at least one hit. Their next turn came from the right and front, close behind other Hurricanes. P/O Zimprich evaded one of the Messerschmitt 109s after him. Shaking it off with an aerobatic shrug, he counterstruck from the rear at 100 yards. The enemy dived but Zimprich did not see the end of the joust.

So the outcome of this engagement was claimed as four Dornier 15s and one Messerschmitt 109 shot down, with probably a further two Messerschmitt 109s. The 11 pilots were Flt Lt Sinclair, Sqn Ldr Hess, Flt Lt Jeffries, P/O Maly, P/O Zimprich, P/O Fechtner, Sgt Kopriva, P/O Goth, P/O Kredba, P/O Janouch and P/O Sterbacek.

During August the usual convoy patrols were maintained daily, so that altogether 1,241 patrols were despatched involving 3,530 individual operational flights of 12 Group.

The night raids centred on Liverpool, Leeds and Sheffield, several aircraft in the Liverpool attacks approaching from the sea and afterwards leaving 12 Group by flying south through Wales. Fires broke out in the Liverpool Docks, while explosions damaged railway yards at Bradford and Leeds. Bombs also fell around Wrexham, Stockport,

Southport, Chesterfield, Doncaster, Coventry, Harleston and in northern Norfolk. The only East Coast aerodrome actually hit was Sherborne where four bombs fell on the runway surface.

Visibility remained poor during the day causing a respite in hostile air activity.

The weather was still far from good overnight on 1–2 September, with patches of fog hampering enemy aircraft which did come. Liverpool and Sheffield felt the fear of bombs bursting at night, while over on the East Coast, Grimsby and Hull had similar experiences. The only other reports coming in referred to minelaying off the Humber Estuary.

Once again, little daytime activity occurred, though at 16.00 hours a raider approached a convoy off Orfordness. 66 Squadron, Red Section chased it out to sea and shot it down six miles north-east of Smith's Knoll. The aircraft turned out to be a Heinkel 111.

On Tuesday 3 September, the first anniversary of the outbreak of war, 12 Group had less night action but more daylight action than on the previous couple of days. Some industrial zones and Hull Docks were bombed but the raids seemed to be spread over a wider geographical spectrum and less concentrated on the large urban areas. This was attributed to the absence of searchlights around city locations. The only searchlights employed anywhere were in the Digby/Boston countryside between 22.56 and 01.03 hours for the purpose of helping night fighters intercept raids. The odd feature of the night's bombing proved to be a total absence of incendiaries on industrial areas, whereas aerodromes received this type of weapon more than high explosives. At Birmingham the Nuffield factory sustained two hits in the vital machine shop and one on a pillbox near the entrance. The raiders loosed their weapons even before any anti-aircraft guns had a chance to open fire. Then by day the Luftwaffe stepped up its offensive and 12 Group were summoned for assistance.

During the morning 310 and 19 Squadrons were despatched to help 11 Group—310 Czech Squadron being in action first. Their ten Hurricanes took off at 09.28 to try to intercept a massive enemy group approaching North Weald from the south-east at 20,000 feet. The estimate was 150 Dornier 215s and Messerschmitt 110s.

Flt Lt J Jeffries was leading B Flight and the squadron. Climbing above the enemy to 20,000 feet he gave the order:

'Line astern.'

Opening their attack from close range, B Flight got in some effective fire. Jeffries gave two short deflection bursts before he singled out one Messerschmitt 110 for a series of outbursts. The Messerschmitt dived away. Thinking it was merely endeavouring to escape, Jeffries dived too but the enemy steepened its dive and blew up on contact with the ground ten miles north of North Weald. At the start of the fight, A Flight under Flt Lt Sinclair were protecting B Flight at about 26,000 feet.

Sgt F Koukal came in behind his leader and managed to meet the enemy from port, from sun and from above. One long burst sent a Messerschmitt 110 spinning down. Koukal then saw a Dornier 215 attacked. It went into a left-hand spin, having its port main plane cut off about a yard from the engine. At 10,000 feet one of the crew got out. It was now nearly an hour after take-off from Duxford.

Sgt Kominek followed Koukal and chose another Messerschmitt 110, hitting it from above, from port and behind and above Koukal. The Messerschmitt 110 Koukal had hit was already doomed. Then Kominek closed to 50 yards on a Dornier 215 and left it limping and diving. The Czech could not claim a victory though as he had to return to the dogfight. P/O Emil Fechtner accounted for a Messerschmitt 110 which strayed right across his sights, and Fechtner saw it strike ground ten miles south-east of North Weald.

The enemy bombers and fighters were at first flying in close herringbone pattern, consisting of alternate lines of 5 Dornier 215s and 5 Messerschmitt 110s. This main formation received further screening by more Messerschmitt 110s flying above it.

As soon as he saw the enemy, A Flight leader Flt Lt Sinclair also ordered his section into line astern and manoeuvred up-sun, still also contriving to help above B Flight. He attacked from the sun and from the rear: a copy book position. Sinclair launched the actual attack the second he saw that the enemy had no Messerschmitt 109s. He destroyed a Messerschmitt 110, two other aircraft, and finally a Dornier 215 by itself. He maintained a prolonged burst and just as he ran out of ammunition it caught alight. This was confirmed by Sgt Furst. After each of these attacks, Sinclair climbed to 22,000–23,000 feet, preserving a couple of thousand feet altitude advantage over the enemy, as well as the use of the sun. After the Germans bombed North Weald, they veered east, the Messerschmitt 110s still just milling around their bombers in no apparent protective tactic.

Sgt B Furst went for the same aircraft as Sinclair at the start, though from the port. After that little initiation rite, Furst stumbled on the rear of another Messerschmitt 110, which he attacked three times—twice from port and once from starboard. His last effort came exactly as the enemy made a severe turn to the right. A single burst from 100 yards and the Messerschmitt 110 took its flaming fuselage down to ground south of Chelmsford. By then Furst was out of ammunition, so that was that.

Sgt Kopriva had a bad hit to his Hurricane and baled out. He floated down safe and sound to survive at least one more day anyway.

With the sky still black with the enemy, though less formally distributed than at the start, the Czech pilot Z M Maly flying Yellow 4 struck home at a Messerschmitt 110, which turned over grotesquely and dived vertically. Maly concluded it must be a total loss as it did not appear to recover while still in his vision. Then he made an attempt on another Messerschmitt 110 but could not claim anything definite. He did notice, however, that both of these Messerschmitts seemed to be replying to his fire very inaccurately. Their lateral firing appeared limited in scope.

So after the main engagements were over, the time read about 10.45 hours. Flt Lt Jeffries had run out of petrol by then so started for home. Koukal put down at North Weald at 11.05 for a quick refuel and then took off again ten minutes later, landing at Duxford soon after the rest at 11.25 hours. The result of the sortie was claimed as 5 Messerschmitt 110s and 1 Dornier 215 destroyed, plus another one of each classed as probables. This was for the loss of one Hurricane and no pilots.

19 Squadron went into action at about the identical time. South of Colchester they found part of the main force of the enemy returning from a raid on the London area. The squadron consisted of eight Spitfires and it operated in sections of two fighters each. Sqn Ldr Pinkham was still climbing to his height of 20,000 feet to patrol Duxford and Debden when he was warned by sector controller of the enemy approaching from the south-east. Later he heard they were over North Weald. At 20,000 feet he saw the explosions and smoke from North Weald, so they had obviously already been there.

Pinkham first saw the Luftwaffe horde heading east. Bombers numbered 50–60 in three group and close box formation. Starting directly astern of the bombers and stretching upwards and backwards through the next 5,000 feet of air space were over a hundred fighters all flying singly. They were turning and twisting, searching and weaving. Above and ahead of the whole lot was one lone fighter.

Pinkham intended to go for this single outrider first of all. But on approach, other enemy fighters left the main group and Pinkham, as Blue 1, took his squadron into two of these instead. He fired at the left-hand one and turned to pursue it. Having lost it, he attacked another almost head-on—only to discover that his guns had jammed. He had fired only ten rounds from each of them.

Blue 2, P/O E Burgoyne, took the right-hand of the pair of fighters—and his starboard gun jammed. He found himself set-on by two Messerschmitt 110s but shrugged them off with a flick from the stick of this Spitfire. He fired at another Messerschmitt until his port gun also jammed. He had fired just 40 rounds from the port and 16 from starboard before the gravity stoppages in each gun.

Green 1 fared better since he had the Spitfire with eight machine-guns. He tried to get at the leader enemy fighter, but it dived towards the bombers for protection. So he picked out a pair of fighters, fired at one from 250 yards, and watched while the enemy struggled to evade. It ended in the familiar dive. He trailed it faithfully down towards the Thames, but eventually it fooled him by flattening out and flying for Whitstable at an altitude of precisely 50 feet—still taking evasive action. On nearing the oyster beds, it turned towards the mouth of the Thames and flew off straight and level. But the battle was not yet won nor lost. Green 1 closed in again and spent the rest of his ammunition from 100 yards. A piece of fabric peeled off the tail of the enemy and the aircraft dived the short distance into the sea. Green 2 stayed with Green 1 ready to help at all stages, but it was not necessary.

Red 1, Flt Sgt G C Unwin, saw the single enemy fighter in front turn towards Blue 1 during Pinkham's attack. Unwin went after it in his Spitfire, closed to 100 yards, and literally blew the port engine out of the wing. The enemy flew on but did not fire any more. Then Red 1 closed in still nearer and fired the remaining rounds of his port gun—his starboard gun having jammed. The next event was the starboard engine of the enemy falling off, so that the aircraft was left powerless in the true sense of the word. One of the crew baled out, and seconds later the aircraft crashed south of Maldon near Battles Bridge. Gravity stoppage had caused the gun of the Spitfire to fail. Red 2, Sgt H A C Roden, fired at random aircraft but could claim no result. He reckoned he was using too much deflection.

Yellow 1 and 2 were the fourth pair. Yellow 1, Sub Lt Blake, was firing at an enemy using a quarter attack from above and on port side. The aircraft swerved violently away and down. Then two Messerschmitt 110s went for Blake, who was also having gun trouble. It was like trying to fight with your arms tied. He had fired only 33 rounds from the port drum when a gravity stoppage put an end to that one. The starboard gun fared even worse. After a mere 14 rounds it jammed due to a deflection plate stoppage. The sorry story of jammings continued with Yellow 2, P/O W Cunningham. He was aiming at the same aircraft as Yellow 1 when he had gravity stoppages after 9 and 4 rounds respectively. That was virtually the end of the action. 19 Squadron shot down 2 Messerschmitt 110s with a further one damaged. Since none of 19 Squadron Spitfires were lost, the total RAF damage was one Hurricane, belonging to Sgt Kopriva. On the debit side, too, the jammings of cannons in most of the Spitfires.

The Luftwaffe entered the second year of war with night raids on 3–4 September starting at 21.30 hours. Bombers made for the Mersey area via South Wales—a sort of back door approach—and the activity went on, except for a lull at 01.30, until 03.00 hours. Liverpool and its docks had hits and fires reflected in the waters of the Mersey near the Wallasey Ferry. Other bombs fell on or near Warrington, Chester, Waterloo and Sealand. Little daylight air action reached 12 Group.

The nightly raids on Liverpool and Manchester regions were really beginning to cause casualties among the civilian population. Private property and, more important, the people living in it—they all suffered in Liverpool, and over at Manchester, the bombers succeeded in hitting the Hope Hospital. The Pendleton oil refineries were badly burned, while telephone cables received damage in many parts of Lancashire. Warrington, Halifax and Wrexham were three other towns on the receiving end, not for the first time in any of their cases.

About 09.42 hours next morning, 5 September, 19 and 310 Squadrons were sent to assist 11 Group. 310 Squadron did not find any intruders, presumably due to being called out late. But 19 Squadron ran into them over the Chatham/Ashford/Medway/Maidstone quadrilateral. Sqn Ldr Pinkham was in command of 5 spitfires in A Flight and 6 in B Flight. They had been despatched to patrol Hornchurch at 15,000 feet. It was Sgt Jennings who spotted some 80 of the Luftwaffe hastening from the west and droning down the Thames Estuary. The estimates of forces were 40 Dornier 215s escorted by 40 Messerschmitt 109s. The Dornier 215s were in vics of 5 stepped up, with the Messerschmitt 109s 5,000 feet higher and just astern. Jennings called up the rest of the squadron in a split second:

'Bandits 15.'

Pinkham detailed A Flight to tackle the fighters and B Flight the bombers. B Flight climbed stubbornly to get in position astern of the Dorniers. They prepared to attack in pairs. Pinkham was flying Blue 1 and led B Flight towards the bombers. Blue 2 lost contact with Blue 1 in the strong sun. Blue 1 was seen heavily engaged with three Dorniers. Blue 2 attacked individually a rear section of three Dornier 215s. Closing from 400 to 150 yards, Blue 2 met experienced fire from a single gun in the port bomber. He noticed fragments falling from the Dornier but he received hits himself and had to break off the conflict. His empenage, elevator and rudder had all suffered and the auxiliary controls were useless. Cannon fire from an unseen rear attacker had caused this serious damage to Blue 2, who somehow staggered home.

Black 1 and 2 then attacked the same Dornier formation from astern. Black 1 opened up from 300 yards and saw the starboard bomber roll away apparently in difficulties. Black 2 had no effect on a port bomber. Then they were both set-on from their rear. The old maxim of the mirror was proving as valid as ever. Black 1 saw a Messerschmitt 109 beneath him. He hit it and the fighter screeched off in distress. Almost as if the machine were crying in pain. Black 2 got a few bursts at another Messerschmitt 109, and saw a further quartet of Messerschmitt 109s which joined in the mêlée.

Green 1 and 2 were intercepted by Messerschmitt 109s as they approached the bombers. Green 1 banked sharply and the pair of Messerschmitts shot past him. He got on the tail of the second and fired a long burst. This Messerschmitt 109 descended graph like to ground level, limping visibly. It hedge-hopped over the Kent countryside with Green 1 sticking fast to its tail, until they were over Ashford town. Then the Messerschmitt climbed, clambered, staggered, up to 800 feet and the pilot baled out. He came down safely in a field, while the Messerschmitt 109 crashed in a garden not far away.

Green 2 singled out one enemy diving to escape an assault from another RAF squadron. He got in bursts at the belly of the enemy, which had turned upside down. Black smoke billowed out, suggesting a victory, but Green 2 himself had to think quickly as two Messerschmitt 109s got sights on him. He escaped by diving and executing an Immelhank turn!

The five Spitfires of A Flight formed a line astern and climbed in a wide circle towards the Messerschmitt 109s at 20,000 feet. The Messerschmitts were joining up for an attack on B Flight, but just as A Flight completed its turn towards the sun, the fighters vanished and failed to reappear—despite A Flight searching for them throughout East Kent.

No-one even knew exactly what happened to Squadron Leader Pinkham. This fine pilot was the holder of the Air Force Cross and an experienced Spitfire flyer. The assumption was that one of the three Dorniers he was attacking got in a fortunate shot. Whatever the precise circumstances, Pinkham was the 19 Squadron casualty of the day: killed in action.

At 15.15 hours, a section of 310 Squadron opened fire on the Luftwaffe at extreme range. During this action, the Czech pilot, P/O Krebda, was wounded.

Liverpool and the Mersey district were the targets during darkness, as well as the Midlands generally. Bombs exploded in the Peak District, and near Manchester, Sheffield, Castle Bromwich, Warrington, Chester and Wigan. Two suburbs of Birmingham bombed were Elmden and Bromsgrove, causing some casualties. Translated that meant people killed and injured. Other bombs further eastward hit Hull, Mablethorpe, Scarborough, Cromer and Yarmouth.

During the day, one flight of 310 Squadron, one flight of 19 Squadron, and 242 Squadron were all ordered to 11 Group but did not manage to contact the enemy. The same was *not* true on the next day. Meanwhile, throughout this first week of September the idea of the Duxford Wing, or Bader Wing, became converted from an abstract or theoretical idea into a practical reality.

5. Douglas Bader was promoted to the rank of Group Captain upon his return from captivity in 1945. He is seen here climbing into the cockpit of a Spitfire in September 1945 prior to leading the 'Victory Flypast' over London.

6. CR-42 Italian aircraft shot down at Orford, Suffolk, 11 November 1940.

CHAPTER 5

First Wing Action

After the customary recent pattern of night raids by the Luftwaffe on the north-west and Midlands, Saturday 7 September dawned. At 08.41 hours, 266 Squadron, Blue Section were ordered to patrol the Yarmouth area, but at 09.00 they spotted a Dornier 215 west of Norwich. They chased it. At first the bomber escaped into the clouds. But they persevered in chasing it right across the North Sea until it was actually over the island of Walcheren. There they came out of the sun and shot it down on to the isle. So much for the morning. The afternoon was due to go down in aviation history as the first offensive patrol by the 12 Group Wing under Douglas Bader.

After the original idea and some discussion between Bader and the other two squadron leaders—Blackwood of 310 Squadron and Lane of 19 Squadron—they flew three or four practice sorties to test out the theory developed by Douglas. Then the Duxford Wing was ready for action. The method of operation was uncomplicated. 242 and 310 Squadrons of Hurricanes took off from Duxford. At the same time, 19 Squadron of Spitfires took off from the satellite station of Fowlmere. There was no joining up over the airfield. Douglas turned straight on to course, climbing quickly, while the other squadrons took up position.

The Hurricane squadrons flew in line astern together, while the Spitfires flew 3/4,000 feet above, behind, and to one side. The intention was that the Spitfires, with their better performance, would guard the Hurricane against interference by Messerschmitt 109s, while they attacked the enemy formations. If there were no enemy fighters, the Spitfires would come down on the bombers after the Hurricanes had broken them up. The Duxford Wing never took more than six minutes to get off the ground and on the way south—and frequently they were off in four minutes. The whole formation arrived over the Thames Estuary at 20,000 feet just twenty minutes after take-off. The Spitfires were then at 23/24,000 feet.

There was no more difficulty in the control of the Wing in the air than of a squadron. The three squadrons were all on the same R/T frequency. An occasional word from Douglas to the other two squadron commanders and then finally his intentions when the enemy were sighted—that was all that was needed. Suggestions from post-war writers that the Big Wing was clumsy in operation are nonsense and without foundation. Indeed they are disproved by the 1941 and subsequent fighter wing operations over France, and later in the Battle of Britain, of course, the Duxford Wing was to number five squadrons, three Hurricane and two Spitfire.

There was one fundamental problem, however, not only with the 12 Group Wing but with 12 Group Squadrons and 11 Group Squadrons. This was due to different reasons although the result was the same: the frequent failure of the 11 Group operations room to get squadrons off the ground in time. Like everyone else, the 11 Group controllers were inexperienced when the Battle started. They did not appreciate that in order for a pilot to be successful, he needs height and position to dominate the battle. The vulnerable, indeed frequently fatal, position for a fighter pilot, is to be climbing with the enemy above him. The German formations used to assemble in the Calais area when the bombers were at 15/17,000 feet. Short-range Messerschmitt 109s joined them and the whole lot proceeded across the Channel towards the London area. This initially precluded a successful interception by any of the 11 Group squadrons based at Manston, Hawkinge, Detling, Gravesend and Redhill, because they were too *near* the coast. A single incident confirms and clarifies this situation: on its very first operational sortie out of Kenley, 616 Squadron lost five out of twelve fighters on the climb without touching the enemy.

So far as the 12 Group Wing was concerned, it seemed to them at Duxford that most times they were sent for as an afterthought, or to do what used to be termed 'the lunch-time patrol' when there was no single aeroplane either German or British in the air at all.

For some reason, the 11 Group controllers would not call squadrons off the ground, and more particularly the 12 Group Wing, until the enemy were at operational height and leaving the French coast. If you look at the map and measure the distance to the 11 Group stations mentioned, the error of this thinking is self-evident. On several occasions, while the Duxford Wing was at readiness, Douglas received telephone calls from the Duxford controller saying:

'Stand by, the Germans are building up over the Calais area.'

Every time Douglas asked:

'Can we take off *now*?'

Every time he received the inevitable answer:

'No, you must wait until 11 Group ask for you.'

Duxford to Tilbury is 43 miles. If the Wing had taken off when the Germans were building up over the Pas de Calais area, Douglas and his team could have been in the Ashford/Tonbridge area under favourable conditions, to control a battle of their own seeking.

Laddie Lucas has summed up Douglas's views on this aspect of the Battle of Britain: 'Douglas's thinking was that he should be able to get these Wings into the air and into the right position to be able to attack the enemy aircraft as they were coming in to their targets, on the approaches to the targets. What he contended was that if you could get these aeroplanes up together, place them right, give them the right information, supply the right commentary, then it was up to Douglas as wing leader to make the best use of it. His basic thinking was not only to get the aeroplanes off together and as quickly as possible, but that proper warning be given and proper decisions regarding control. The difficulty with the Duxford Wing was probably to get off the ground in time to discharge the tactics that Douglas believed to be necessary to fulfil his role. Too often he found himself climbing up as hard as he could bloody well go, while the enemy were already coming in–so he would have lost all the advantage of height and sun and so on.'

Douglas disagreed with the attitude of fighting the Battle of Britain on a local level, rather as a private 11 Group affair, and an order from the AOC 11 Group susbsequently available makes it clear that in his mind his fears were fully justified. This was Park's peculiar instruction in force from 19 August 1940, which went against so much of what Douglas felt to be the best approaches. It is worth quoting in full, so that Bader's reaction to it can be completely understood.

NO 11 GROUP INSTRUCTIONS TO CONTROLLERS NO 4
From: Air Officer Commanding, No 11 Group, Royal Air Force.
To: Group Controllers and Sector Commanders, for Sector Controllers.
Date: 19 August 1940

The German Air Force has begun a new phase in air attacks, which have been switched from coastal shipping and ports on to inland objectives. The bombing attacks have for several days been concentrated against aerodromes, and especially fighter aerodromes, on the coast and inland. The following instructions are issued to meet the changed conditions:

a) Despatch fighters to engage large enemy formations over land or within gliding distance of the coast. During the next two or three weeks, we cannot afford to lose pilots through forced landings in the sea;

b) Avoid sending fighters out over the sea to chase reconnaissance aircraft or small formations of enemy fighters;

c) Despatch a pair of fighters to intercept single reconnaissance aircraft that come inland. If clouds are favourable, put a patrol of one or two fighters over an aerodrome which enemy aircraft are approaching in clouds;

d) Against mass attacks coming inland, despatch a minimum number of squadrons to engage enemy fighters. Our main object is to engage enemy bombers, particularly those approaching under the lowest cloud cover;

e) If all our squadrons around London are off the ground engaging enemy mass attacks, ask No 12 Group or Command Controller to provide squadrons to patrol aerodromes Debden, North Weald, Hornchurch;

f) If heavy attacks have crossed the coast and are proceeding towards aerodromes, put a squadron, or even the sector training flight, to patrol under clouds over each sector aerodrome;

g) No 303 (Polish) Squadron can provide two sections for patrol of inland aerodromes, especially while the older squadrons are on the ground refuelling, when enemy formations are flying over land;

h) No 1 (Canadian) Squadron can be used in the same manner by day as other fighter squadrons.

NOTE: Protection of all convoys and shipping in the Thames Estuary are excluded from this instruction (paragraph (a)).

Sqd K R Park
Air Vice-Marshal
Commanding,
No 11 Group
Royal Air Force

In Douglas's decided and considered view, these instructions revealed some serious errors of thinking in air warfare. Paragraph (e) was the fatal one, he maintained, as the best way to protect aerodromes was not to fly overhead waiting for an attack, but to go and intercept the enemy where he wanted. Stop them reaching our airfields. This same argument applied to paragraphs (c) and (f). Finally, paragraph (a) at one stroke precluded successful interception by any squadron south of the River Thames.

Lord Dowding made two vital contributions to the defeat of the Luftwaffe in the summer of 1940. During his pre-war command, he had laid down radar coverage of the south of England so that we had early warning of the Germans intentions: secondly, he had persuaded the War Cabinet against sending more RAF fighters to a defeated France in May 1940.

Instead of assuming control and direction of the air defence of Britain, which was the C-in-C's job, Dowding left the conduct of the battle to a subordinate Group Commander, A V M Park of No 11 Group. Dowding had already increased the number of squadrons in 11 Group, making it the strongest in Fighter Command. Keith Park fought the Battle of Britain, not Dowding. He fought it under the disadvantage of being too near the enemy to deploy the strength which Dowding had given him. His problem was compounded by his operations room displaying a map of 11 Group territory only. In other words, Park was fighting an 11 Group battle which should have been a Fighter Command battle.

A map of the whole of England lay on the plotters' table at Fighter Command. It showed every Fighter airfield, with the location and state of readiness of every squadron on the board above it. The difference was paramount. A controller at the Fighter Command operations room would have seen the enemy position as it was plotted. With the whole picture spread out in front of him, he would instantly have realised the need to scramble squadrons from the further away airfields *first* against the enemy. First, not last.

This would have provided the classic air defence in depth so desperately needed to make life easier for controllers and less costly for pilots. 11 Group controllers with their limited operations room facilities would have given place to Fighter Command ones with the map of England in front of them. 11 Group controllers were being harassed by enemy raiders almost overhead, which they were trying to intercept with only 11 Group squadrons available. The Fighter Command controllers would have had time to see the problem in its entirety. It was in this context that the Duxford Wing came into being, indeed for these very reasons. Leigh-Mallory saw the whole situation with clarity from his 12 Group headquarters. So did Douglas. Easy for them, say the critics, they were not in the so-called front line. Quite right. But this highlights the great error: the front line should have embraced the whole of Fighter Command and not just 11 Group.

If ever Dowding should have seen the light it was at the end of August, when the changing pattern of the German assault became clear beyond doubt. Vast enemy formations were to be seen congregating over the Pas-de-Calais. London must be the target. Surely the Commander-in-Chief, with his great reputation and the full resources of his headquarters and operations room, would now take over control of the battle from his 11 Group Commander. In the event, he did not. A tired man with neither the authority nor the full available resources was left to continue the struggle. It was as though General Montgomery left a Corps Commander to fight the Battle of Alamein and told him to call on other corps commanders for assistance if necessary. The Battle of Britain was won by the efforts of tired but resolute controllers and the immense courage of 11 Group pilots. Properly exploited, the 12 Group Wing could have provided the spearhead against the enemy formations, creating havoc amongst them and giving the 11 Group pilots time to gain height and position to continue the destruction. To stress the irony of the 11 Group situation, squadrons sometimes had to climb northwards *away* from the enemy, to try and gain tactical advantage. At the top level of Fighter Command, there seemed an inability to grasp the basic and proved rules of air fighting. This is what Douglas felt then and still feels three or four decades later.

12 Group introduced its report on the first five Wing patrols with the following comments, setting the scene in the context of 7 September 1940:

'Experience has shown that with the mass attacks on London and the South of England, the enemy has used not only larger formations of bombers but very considerably larger formations of protecting fighters. In view of this, when No 12 Group have been asked to protect North Weald and Hornchurch Aerodromes, it was considered wholly inadequate to send up single squadrons for this purpose and therefore a Wing has been employed. Up to the present, five such operations have taken place. Definite roles have been allotted to the squadrons on each occasion, with the general idea of having Spitfire Squadrons above the Hurricane Squadrons so that the former could attack enemy fighters and prevent their coming down to protect their bombers, whilst the remainder of the Wing break up and destroy the enemy bombers.'

Johnnie Johnson described the situation on 7 September rather more dramatically in his highly informed book *Full Circle*.

'On September 7, following Hitler's declaration that London would suffer as reprisals for Bomber Command raids against Berlin, Goering switched his bombers from RAF sector stations, and other airfields, to London and its sprawling docks. Towards five o'clock on that evening, more than three hundred bombers, and many hundreds of fighters, rose from their airfields across the Channel, swarmed into a dozen formations and, without feint or decoy, crossed the straits in two broad waves and headed for the capital. Because of their height, above 20,000 feet, and a stiff head wind, the bombers took a long time to reach London, but although RAF controllers found it easier than usual to intercept, the enemy fighter escorts seemed bigger than ever. There were so many enemy fighters, layered up to 30,000 feet, that a Spitfire pilot said it was like looking up the escalator at Piccadilly Circus.'

'Near Cambridge the Duxford Wing of two Hurricane and one Spitfire squadrons had been at readiness all day and Bader, anxious to lead thirty-six fighters into action for the first time, had been agitating for hours about getting into the air. At last they were scrambled . . . '

The Wing was ordered off from Duxford at about 16.55 hours to patrol North Weald. The altitude quoted was 10,000 feet. Control told Bader: '100 bandits approaching you from the east.' Arriving at North Weald on the 15,000 feet level, they noticed AA fire to the east and saw a quantity of enemy aircraft at 20,000 feet. Bader immediately advised Duxford of the sighting and obtained permission to engage the enemy. He took the decision to attack with 242, 310 and 19 Squadrons knowing that such a move must have been more successful had the Wing been at 25,000 feet. The element of surprise was lost to them and they endured the added disadvantage of attacking the bombers knowing that there were Messerschmitt 109s above them and in the sun so that while pressing home any attack they would have to try to keep an eye behind them at the same time if they were to survive. No wonder Douglas and other pilots of the Wing grew impatient at a policy which put precious aircrew at so substantial a hazard from the outset.

Bader opened his Hurricane throttle to 674 boost and climbed for all he and the fighter were worth. The enemy aircraft were proceeding north over the Thames Estuary. The result of the full throttle climbing to get level with the enemy made the whole fighter force struggle out of necessity--so the attack could not be pressed home with the weight of the 36 aeroplanes at Bader's disposal. But he had to engage quickly or not at all.

He turned left to cut off the enemy and arrived on the beam slightly in front with only Red 2. Bader was flying Red 1, and Sub Lt Cork flew Red 2. Bader opened with a very short beam squirt from 100 yards, aimed at enemy aircraft flying in sections of three line astern in a large rectangle. He turned with Cork, who also fired with him, and sat under the tails of the back section at 50 yards, pulling up the nose and giving short squirts at the middle back aeroplane. This was a Messerschmitt 110 and it started smoking, preparatory to catching fire.

Even before attacking the enemy and whilst actually still climbing to meet them, Cork and Bader received a lot of cross-fire from enemy bombers, which kept in perfect formation. At the same time, they were set on by enemy fighters, who had had the advantage of 3,000–4,000 feet in altitude.

Cork broke away slightly to the right of Bader's section and fired at a Dornier 215 on the tail end of the group. It followed the usual destruction sequence of port engine afire and a vertical crash-dive.

Before Douglas could see the result of his opening action, he saw the warning outline of a yellow nose in his mirror. The Messerschmitt 109 was on his tail slightly above and as Bader turned there was suddenly a big bang in his cockpit from a bullet—presumably an explosive one. It came in through the right-hand side of the fuselage, touched the map case, knocked the corner off the undercarriage selector quadrant and finished up against the petrol priming pump.

Having executed a quick, steep, diving turn, Bader found a Messerschmitt 110 alone just below him. He attacked this from dead astern and above. The Messerschmitt could not combat the accurate Bader fire and went into a steepish straight dive, finishing up in flames in a field just north of a railway line west of Wickford and due north of Thameshaven. The first Messerschmitt 110 attacked by Bader had been confirmed as diving down and crashing by another pilot, although Douglas himself had not witnessed it. So that made a couple of Messerschmitts to the Wing leader: an example to the rest of them. Apart from the bullet in the cockpit, Bader's Hurricane also sustained hits in several places by bomber fire and twice by escorting Messerschmitt 109s.

Just after Cork had destroyed the Dornier, he was set on from the rear by an enemy fighter and hit in the starboard mainplane. So he broke away downwards and backwards—and nearly collided head-on with a Messerschmitt 110. This was always a danger, and collisions did happen with fatal results to both parties. Cork pressed for a brief burst before pulling away to avoid the collision and he saw the front of the Messerschmitt cabin break up and the aircraft take a vertical dive. Two of the crew baled out. Cork followed the machine down. It was stalling and then diving again alternately.

While Cork continued his vigil, a Messerschmitt 109 went for his rear. One shot penetrated the side of his hood, hit the bottom of the reflector sight and then the bullet-proof windscreen. 'As I could not see very well, I broke away downwards in a half-roll and lost vision of the enemy machine.' Not really surprising with glass in his eyes. Somehow he kept on flying, having accounted for a Dornier 215 and a Messerschmitt 110. When he landed, his Hurricane was so shattered with enemy fire that it was not considered flyable.

A great friend of Douglas Bader, Denis Crowley-Milling was flying as his Red 3. The time was between 17.00 and 17.15 now and they were still in the thick of this dogfight, started from a poorly placed position.

Red 3 saw a lot of the cross-fire from other bombers as he flew in to meet a force just above the AA fire. But he had to snap off due to a rear thrust by a Messerschmitt 110. Red 3 banked left sharply and then came in again at the bombers. He spotted a Messerschmitt 110 just behind the last bomber. He hit its port engine with a four-second burst and saw the starboard one smoking, too. At that instant he was shot at from behind by a Messerschmitt 109. His Hurricane received a shell in the radiator, another in the left aileron, and a third behind the pilot's seat. No-one could deny he was lucky to be alive. He piloted the Hurricane down from 18,000 -20,000 feet to a crash-landing near Chelmsford. In fact he had destroyed the Messerschmitt 110 which he attacked.

Irrespective of individual actions, the rest of the engagement continued its inexorable pattern, as if moving to some predetermined choreography in an aerial ballet.

After Bader had gone in originally, Flt Lt G Ball as Yellow 1 positioned himself a few thousand feet higher than nearby enemy aircraft, and opened against a Messerschmitt 110. Messerschmitt 109s caught him by the tail, however, and he realised that by now he was utterly alone, with no friendly fighters in immediate sight. He saw a second 110 and closed from 300 to 75 yards. It caught fire soon after his running attack from above and behind. He fired on three or four other aircraft but they were impossible to engage for long owing to the horde of fighters buzzing around their bombers.

Ball actually followed the formation out to sea, picking off a 110 en route. Both engines of the enemy were smoking but a 109 got on his tail and he had to give up further pursuit. Although the enemy fired on him sporadically, Ball found their aim very wild and he was not hit at all.

Sgt R Lonsdale followed Ball in to the original affray. As he flew into the attack approximately level with the enemy bombers, Messerschmitt 110s came down and broke up their particular formation. The enemy fighters kept good grouping but for that very reason were fairly easily avoided. Three 110s dived for Lonsdale but again he twisted out of trouble.

Then he went for the bombers by himself. The sun was on his starboard side as he selected a Dornier 215 to attack from live astern. After a diminishing range from 350 to 80 yards, the Hurricane's fire stopped the port engine and smouldered the starboard one. While in the thick of this attack, Lonsdale suddenly found his Hurricane being bounced about a lot by the slipstream of the bomber. He carried on his attack from slightly below to get out of its line. The Dornier 215 gradually dropped back from the formation and started gliding down at about 120 mph. Lonsdale had given it a full 15 seconds of firing and at this stage ran out of ammunition. Despite this, he followed the bomber down for some distance until it disappeared from sight. Another Hurricane hit it as it glided on.

Flt Lt D ff Powell-Sheddon led Blue Section and estimated enemy forces at 50 bombers in tight grouping line astern with a strong guard of Messerschmitt 110s and yellow-nosed Messerschmitt 109s. The noses also had some silver on them as camouflage. Powell-Sheddon climbed to 22,000 feet to have a go at the fighters, having lost sight of Bader and the section in front. The other members of Blue Section had also become separated from him. But this was no more than typical of the style and pattern of such a dogfight.

Powell-Sheddon chased several enemy aircraft but did not engage any for ten minutes. Volumes of jet smoke were cascading up from Thameshaven oil refineries. Miles above Thameshaven, Powell-Sheddon saw a Hurricane being chased by a Messerschmitt 109. They swerved right in front of him, a mere 100 yards ahead. He gave an instinctive deflection squirt at the Messerschmitt 109 as it passed, and it then turned left and again crossed his path at the same range. He repeated the squirt and got on its tail. As the Messerschmitt 109 was firing at the Hurricane, Blue 1 was aiming at the German from a few feet above and only 50 yards. He could see his bullets finding their mark and saw pieces ripped from the Hurricane. He got in the enemy slipstream, ceased fire, eased slightly to one side, and fired again.

The Messerschmitt 109 got the Hurricane, which went down with smoke streaming. Then the Messerschmitt 109 itself hung in the air for a few seconds before falling forward in a vertical dive. A tail of smoke etched its descent in the sky. It vanished into the dense blackness over Thameshaven. As it seemed to be in flames and out of control, the Messerschmitt 109 could be claimed for Powell-Sheddon.

The speed with which the Wing went into action could be deduced from the time of these attacks: 17.10/17.15 hours. Only a quarter of an hour or so after actual take-off. Blue 2 was P/O P Bush. He went for a Heinkel 111 but had to break off because of rear attacks from a Messerschmitt 110. He executed in turn an astern attack on another Messerschmitt 110, which he damaged badly. Two good bursts from 250 to 50 yards caused these hits.

A few minutes later, P/O H Tamblyn as Blue 3 destroyed a Messerschmitt 110 at 17.20 hours. It became a total conflagration. Tamblyn next went after a 109 at 150 yards. Evidence suggested he had hit it lethally as it veered gently to the right and began to go down. It was one of the special yellow-nose squadron. Tamblyn felt an effect of slipstream from both these encounters but managed to control his Hurricane.

Green 1 now and P/O D S Turner—a favourite of Douglas Bader. He was in the last section to attack and as he approached he saw a Messerschmitt 110 already in flames. This was as a result of one of the Red Section hits. While hitting a 110 and watching his bullets tear at the fuselage, Turner was in turn fired at by a 109. He outmanoeuvred the fighter and got a good burst into it. The Messerschmitt flicked into a dive. Turner went for some bombers next, and before being driven off by 109s, he got in a snap shot or two. Nothing for it after that but to head for Duxford.

Still 17.20 hours: Gardner was the name of the pilot of Green 4. He saw 30 Heinkels plus more bombers and many Messerschmitt 109s. He noticed some Spitfires already in the fray. On entering the mêlée in sharp zigzags, he found it very difficult to distinguish friend from foe—certainly in the instants available for decisions. But he did recognise a Dornier which started to circle and dive. Gardner went too and discovered he had another Hurricane along with him.

At 5,000 feet Gardner got in three short bursts from 250 to 50 yards, stopping the port engine and bursting the oil tank. The crew baled out and the Dornier crashed in a field about three miles northwest of Shell Haven. Gardner got a hole in his wing and engine cowling but managed to land early at 17.45 hours.

A Dornier 215 singled out by Black 1, P/O M Stansfield, loosed off about 50 rounds of machine-gun fire at him, but fortunately missed his Hurricane. Coming up from below it, he caught the bomber in the port beam. The enemy went into a roll and then attempted a second one—but this was too low to be executed. It dived into the ground, the pilot having misjudged the altitude.

So much for 242 Squadron. They took off at 16.55. They landed at 17.55. An hour to remember. They lost two Hurricanes, force-landed in Essex, but both pilots were safe—that was the main thing. Five fighters became temporarily unserviceable through bullet holes.

The Czechs followed Douglas and 242 Squadron in line astern. Flt Lt G Sinclair was leading 310 (Czech) Squadron, A Flight, and traced Calla leader into an up-sun position. He put A Flight into line astern to go for Messerschmitt 110s behind the bombers. Having seen 242 Squadron attacking the bombers, Sinclair took as his target a Messerschmitt 110 with full deflection shot. Another burst on another Messerschmitt 110. He climbed into the sun and gave a third Messerschmitt 110 prolonged attention. The port engine ceased to function, but then Sinclair ran out of ammunition so had to call off further offensive acts.

Sinclair was Red 1, P/Sgt B Furst Red 2 and Sgt Seda Red 3.

Furst fired at one of the Messerschmitt 110s attacked by Sinclair and then followed him. Seda did the same. But Furst failed to find Sinclair again. Furst next hit a 110 and left it smoking from the port engine over Whitstable. This was a far cry from the days of peace and the famous oysters. The enemy glided down in turns towards the east, with both his engines failing to function. But Furst could only claim a probable success.

He was more definite a few minutes afterwards. He trailed a group of enemy bombers north of Canterbury. Far below the cathedral made its cross as it had done in plain view over the centuries. Furst found himself 50 yards behind a Messerschmitt 109. One burst hit the Messerschmitt. But not before the pilot somehow baled out. Furst was waylaid by two Messerschmitt 110s and had to beat a hasty retreat.

Sgt Seda followed Sinclair as he led their section in a curve towards the enemy bombers. Next moment, he saw a Messerschmitt 110 only 50 yards ahead of him. He fired. White smoke made parallel trails from the engines but Seda did not see the Messerschmitt crash. Hence: one damaged Messerschmitt 110.

Again at the five-minute spell from 17.15–17.20 hours, P/O S Janouch was leading Yellow Section, A Flight at 25,000 feet over Grays Thurrock. He took Yellow Section towards enemy fighters, level out of the sun. Then they had to transfer efforts to a bomber force. But the fighters wedged between the bombers and themselves. A Messerschmitt 110 appeared just in front of Janouch's windscreen and tried desperately to escape by going into a glide. Janouch fired five bursts at 400 to 50 yards, the middle burst producing smoke from both engines. Yellow 2 and 3 also went for this 110, but only Yellow 3 got in a burst. These other two of Yellow Section saw two men bale out of the aircraft. Janouch climbed to regain an operational height and joined another squadron of Hurricanes, before being called on to land.

Flt Lt J Jeffries led B Flight of 310 Squadron. He climbed into the sun, fired all his rounds at one fighter, and saw scraps of metal careering off it. But he was slightly out of range and was just unable to get any closer—so could not clinch his attack. Jeffries was flying Blue 1. P/O V Goth came in behind at Blue 2, with F/O J F Boulton as Blue 3. Goth had an adventurous few minutes.

Jeffries told them to attack scattered enemy singly. A Messerschmitt 110 selected by Goth joined the bombers and was insisting on orbiting above it. He delivered his fire from the sun and the rear. He dived on the Messerschmitt 110 from the port, opening fire at 200 yards. By 50 yards range, the enemy was emitting a heavy smoke pall and Goth saw the cockpit break up in the air. The

Messerschmitt went mechanically unconcious, falling vertically towards the Thames Estuary area between Southend and Foulness Island.

As Goth broke away, he felt that his Hurricane had been hit. Then another enemy was upon him. A dogfight barked out. Enemy fire ceased and he saw that the port engine was badly struck. The enemy machine lurched right then dramatically left, apparently set for a spin. Goth saw the air gunner hit as the port engine flamed. They were both over the sea by this stage.

Goth could not see anything more as his cockpit was oozing with oil. His engine started cutting off. The glycol tank was pouring forth white smoke. Then the engine cut off completely. Goth shut the throttle and dived towards the coast. Somehow he saw through all the usual obstacles. He landed with his undercarriage up about two miles south-east of Maldon in Essex.

Blue 3 had a less dramatic outcome. F/O J F Boulton made his attacks between 17.15 and 17.35 hours. During the first of two encounters, he fired at a Messerschmitt 110 over the Estuary from below and behind. No results. Then he espied a Heinkel 111 heading in a south-easterly course over Kent. After crossing the coast, he carried out a couple of stern attacks at 15,000 feet. He fired all his remaining rounds at the Heinkel 111 and the port engine smoked. The Heinkel lost height remorselessly and never recovered any aeronautical composure, crashing into the Channel not far from the Goodwin Sands. Another Hurricane confirmed this gain.

Green 1 and 2 were the last two Czechs reporting. P/O E Fechtner as Green 1 fired at a force of bombers from below. He was on the port side of his section and caused the middle of a bomber engine to smoke. A Messerschmitt 110 appeared and he fired at this one. The Messerschmitt gave a little climb, lurched into a wounded spin, and descended into the mass of dense smoke over the oil refineries. An enemy bullet hit Fechtner's main tank but luckily for him it did not explode, nor was he hurt.

While P/O S Zimprich at Green 2 was en route for Dorniers, he diverted to a Messerschmitt 110 below him. Firing from 300 to 50 yards, he hit the port engine and the Messerschmitt 110 glided groundwards.

He followed another Messerschmitt 110 just above the beachline, only 400 yards above the blackness rising from the bombed oil tanks. The aircraft folded up on the left, crumpled, and crashed into the inferno. An enemy bullet struck the 'footstep' of Zimprich's Hurricane.

Eight Spitfires of 19 Squadron accompanied 242 and 310 Squadrons. They saw a force of 20 bombers escorted by 50 fighters flying east at 15,000 feet. 19 Squadron was the last of the trio to attack, being 5,000 feet lower than this enemy formation.

While still on the climb to attack, they met a Messerschmitt 110 diving past them at a substantial speed—with Red Leader, A Flight after it. Two Hurricanes were also in tow. All five members of A Flight fired at this enemy which met its end a mile or so east of Hornchurch and south of a railway line. The crew of two baled out but one parachute failed to open . . . The other man landed in a field and appeared to be taken a prisoner by two women from a nearby house.

Sqn Ldr Lane was Red 1, with Sgt Jennings Red 2 and F/Sgt Unwin Red 3. Red 1 and 2 plus Yellow 1 (Flt Sgt Lawson) returned to base as the main combat had literally vanished.

Red 3 mislaid the others but on climbing to 25,000 feet found and joined a Hurricane squadron. He was led into a force of some 60 enemy machines, bombers and fighters mixed about equally. The Hurricanes were busy with the bombers, while Red 3 suddenly found himself surrounded by Messerschmitt 109s. He fired at, and hit, five. Two went down. He then extricated his Spitfire, shadowing an enemy group from a great height. This force was at 20,000 feet and being attacked accurately by AA fire which scored two decisive strikes. Red 3 used up his ammunition on a batch of unescorted bombers.

Yellow 2, P/O Cunningham, also lost the rest of the squadron and joined up with Hurricanes. They flew east and aimed for 24 Heinkel 111s. Yellow 2 selected and fired at one Heinkel 111, set it ablaze, attacked again from below, and finally saw it die some ten miles inland from Deal or Ramsgate—he was not sure which at that moment and it did not really matter.

B Flight of 19 Squadron were out of range of the enemy by the time they had staggered up to the level of the enemy and Blue 1 and 2 had to return to base without firing. Blue 3 cottoned on to another squadron and shot down a Messerschmitt 110 into the sea off Margate. Blue 1 and 2 were Flt Lt Clouston and F/Sgt Steere. Blue 3 was P/O Dolezal.

So summarising the results of the first Wing patrol in adverse conditions, the three squadrons under Douglas Bader inflicted this damage: 20 destroyed; 5 probables; 6 damaged. Our losses were 4 destroyed, 1 damaged with 1 pilot killed/missing and 1 wounded. They heard later that P/O Benzie was dead.

Analysed by squadrons the results were 242 Squadron destroyed 10; probables 2; damaged 3. 310 Squadron destroyed 5; probables 3; damaged 3. 19 Squadron destroyed 5.

There was one day's respite before the next Wing action, probably due to showers and cloud conditions. Meanwhile the enemy restricted itself to night raids.

Only 28 hostile aircraft were plotted in 12 Group throughout the night of 7–8 September. Apart from two or three sporadic raids over the Mersey area, activity was chiefly confined to East Anglia and the Humber. Bombs actually fell near Liverpool, Birkenhead, Kirton-in-Lindsey, Spilsby, Northampton, Bircham Newton and Mildenhall. The sole daytime ventures by the enemy were of a reconnaissance nature, almost as if they were licking their undoubted wounds of the previous day and considering the next move to make.

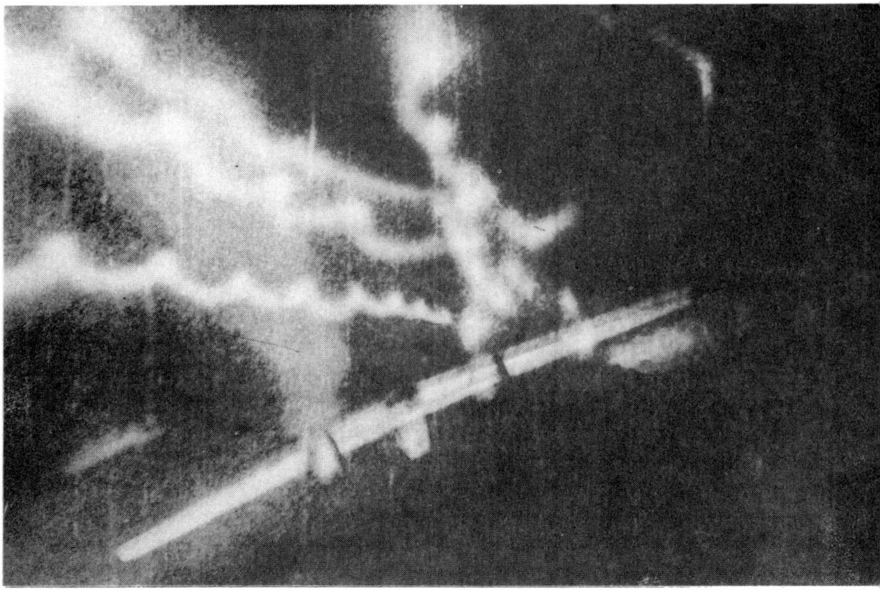

7. Aerial combat with Messerschmitt 110. The British fighter has put concentrated fire into the port engine and damaged the port wing.

8. Heinkel 111 over the Thames and Silvertown district of London, as seen from another German aircraft.

9. Pilots leaping from their lorry and dashing to the waiting Spitfires.

10. Hurricanes in formation above the clouds on their way to engage raiders reported heading for London.

CHAPTER 6

Second Wing Action

Slight night-time activity again, including a couple of raids around the Mersey, one of which dropped a stick or two of bombs near Wrexham. Small-scale bombing sorties over East Anglia had objectives at Mildenhall and St Ives—Hunts not Cornwall.

Once more, Johnnie Johnson sets the scene for the second Duxford Wing patrol that afternoon:

'On September 9 the Luftwaffe repeated their tactics of the 7th, sending over two waves in quick succession, with fighter forces ranging ahead and on the flanks of the main formations. The Germans were after London and aeroplane factories at Brooklands, but had little success, for one raid was met, as Park intended, well forward, and the bombs were scattered through much cloud near Canterbury.'

As usual Bader ventilated his feelings to his sector commander, Wing Commander Woodhall, about getting into the air; Woodhall pressed the 12 Group controller who, in turn, inquired of his opposite number at 11 Group whether the Duxford Wing was required. Eventually they were scrambled, and once radio contact was established between controller and wing leader, Woodhall said: 'Will you patrol between North Weald and Hornchurch, angels twenty?' Never one at the best of times for blind obedience to orders, Woodhall's 'will you' was not lost on Bader, and this intimacy between the two men was important, because it had wide repercussions on the authority of wing leaders.

Woodhall, affectionately known as 'Woodie', was a veteran of the Kaiser's War, and was one of the best and most trusted controllers in Fighter Command. His calm and measured tones seemed full of confidence and assurance, and he was fully aware of the limitations of radar, which, at this time, was often distorted by enemy jamming. Woodhall knew that his wing leader was in the best position to judge how and when to attack, and therefore his controlling technique was to advise rather than to instruct.

Bader, climbing hard to the south, figured that once again the Germans would come out of the evening sun, so he forgot about Hornchurch and the height and climbed high over Staines, thirty miles from Hornchurch and well within 11 Group's preserves. He was just in time to position his wing between the sun and two big shoals of bombers accompanied by the usual pack of 109s.

It was at about 17.40 hours that Douglas saw the enemy coming in from about 15 miles south-west of them and at the same height of 22,000 feet. Leading the same three squadrons as two days earlier, 33 fighters this time instead of 34, he turned to head them off, while climbing all the time to gain advantage of altitude. The enemy was in two large rectangular formations; one of approximately 60, then a space of a quarter-mile of sky, followed by a further 60, with a 500 feet step-up between the two groups.

Bader radioed Duxford to tell 19 Squadron of Spitfires to climb up and protect their tails and then he turned 242 and 310 Squadrons in above the front bomber formation—nearly down sun and 1,000 feet above them. Bader had told 242 Squadron to attack in loose line astern and to try to break up the enemy formation. He was aiming at the leader, who was slightly in front of the leading section.

As he turned 242 directly above the bombers, Bader noticed some fighters diving out of the sun between the twin enemy bomber forces, but he dismissed them as friendly fighters. Actually they turned out to be Messerschmitt 109s which went for 242 on its turn. The squadron retaliated though so Bader was not really worried by them.

Bader followed his plan by diving on the leader, with a two-seconds' burst at point blank distance. Douglas continued his dive past the enemy, through and under the formation. He pulled up underneath them, intending to give his victim another squirt from below, but saw white smoke misting from both wings. Then he saw the machine roll over on its back in a dive. He did not bother to watch it further, but Sgt Brimble and P/O Bush both saw at least one person bale out as it descended in a flame-trail. Douglas could not be sure at that second whether it was a Dornier 215 or 17—he admitted to finding it hard to tell the difference.

P/O Willie McKnight was Bader's faithful Red 2. At 17.45 they were south of the Thames now. McKnight flew into the enemy from 1,000 feet above and on his left beam. He broke to the left to go for the protecting enemy fighters. He got behind one of them and sent it up—or down—in flames. Next he got between two enemy attacking his Hurricane. He opened up at one and the machine shed metallic fragments as it dived to earth. But the German at Willie's rear also opened up and blew off his left aileron. He saw his second Messerschmitt 109 quite out of control. McKnight survived even with his missing aileron.

While Douglas manoeuvred into the sun and did his dive on the leading section, Flt Lt G Ball, leading Yellow Section, took his Hurricane at the second enemy section. He dived through the enemy, pulled up, and did a frontal attack on the leading section, hoping to split them up. He saw no effect from his best laid plan, but he did see a Messerchmitt 109 buzzing on his tail. He wriggled around to reverse their relative positions and firing from 300 to 100 yards witnessed the spectacle of the 109 literally blowing up in mid-air. Satisfying yet sobering. Ball got only one enemy bullet in his Hurricane.

Blue Leader was another veteran of 242 Squadron: Flt Lt G ff Powell-Sheddon. He was B Flight and Blue Section was the third in 242 Squadron. But before the attack even, the sections became open and irregular, with Bader still out in front! Powell-Sheddon, Blue 1, saw Bader drop his nose and head ramlike for the first 30 enemy. Blue 1 admits to making a mess of his first attempt. He tried to get the leader but overshot and could not open fire.

Then he made a steep climb, turned swiftly, and roared at the bombers again—aiming this time at the second leader. Three seconds at 50 yards and he saw the bullets striking the engine nacelle and the wing. He passed over the enemy about 20 feet from it and broke away in another steep climb. Glancing back, he saw the port engine afire. The bomber lagged behind and fell out of the formation, like a runner dropping behind with cramp.

Powell-Sheddon then lost sight of it for a very good and immediate reason. He lost control of his Hurricane. His starboard aileron control cable had been shot clean through and broken. By a bit of superior piloting, he managed to regain some semblance of control and set his nose towards home, with the enemy lost amid the mixture of haze and cloud. But he was credited with the destruction of one Dornier 215. The dogfight went on.

Bader remained under the formation he was attacking—some 300 feet below them. He pulled up periodically, squirting various aeroplanes at very close range. But although he damaged them, he saw no definite results. He did see another Dornier in the front diving slowly in a left-handed shallow spiral, obviously out of action and smoking. This was the Second Leader shot down by Powell-Sheddon.

Suddenly Douglas discovered salvoes of bombs falling all around his Hurricane, so he decided to ease his stick away to the side. The bomber formation veered to the right and made off south-east. They were still in formation, about 20 of them, but they had left a lot of stragglers all over the sky—some damaged and others going slowly even for bombers. It was obvious that their bombing was absolutely indiscriminate. London was covered by a 3,000 feet layer of broken cloud, thick haze up to 9,000 feet, and clear above. They were bombing from 20,000 feet and so far as Douglas could see, south of the Thames, around London Bridge, and in the Battersea area. Douglas went on with his plan of chasing the stragglers and firing short close-range bursts at them to conserve ammunition. But finally it was all gone. Before he left, he saw a very large bomber with a single rudder flying home quite slowly and sedately. He attacked it by flying very close and then turning across it to put it off its stride. But it took no notice and did not even fire at him. There was nothing more he could do. His tally was one Dornier destroyed and several damaged.

Flying close to Powell-Sheddon as Blue 2, P/O R Bush sighted the enemy first over the Thames near London Bridge. He took part in a line astern attack from the sun on these bombers. Evading a Messerschmitt 109, he found a 110 and shot it down, the aircraft breaking up like some miniature toy machine. But this was not child's play. Fire from behind by another 110 prompted Bush to execute a neat half-roll and call it a day.

Blue 3 was P/O F Tamblyn. He saw some 200 enemy altogether, a daunting sight. This was at 17.35 hours now. As he approached, he observed five Messerschmitt 110s detach themselves and turn in a right hand circle towards the rear of the enemy formation. Their altitude measured 22,000 feet. Tamblyn turned into an astern assault and noticed a Hurricane set a 110 on fire. And in turn, on the tail of the Hurricane another 110 dogged it with tentative thoroughness. A long burst at the Hurricane did not seem to do any damage. Tamblyn opened at the 110 whenever it straightened up—and after one of these bursts both engines lit up. Meanwhile Tamblyn also noticed a Hurricane with its port wing folding up and another fighter—also taken to be a Hurricane—in a similar predicament.

Tamblyn flew to the far side of the formation and climbed again. He saw a 110 making across him in a steep turn so gave a brief burst. From dead astern he then devoted 7 seconds to the same aircraft which crumpled into a fairly steep dive. The Hurricane Blue 3 followed it down and watched it crash in front of a cricket clubhouse within a hundred yards or so of another crashed aircraft. There were many star-like spots on the ground, which could have been the results of incendiary bombs.

Sgt E Richardson as Green 1 found a Dornier 215. Six seconds of firing from 300 to 200 yards brought smoke to its starboard engine and main-plane. The sergeant pilot broke away at 200 yards. Regaining position 300 yards behind it, he closed to 100 yards, seeing smoke from the port engine after his second 6-second burst. Richardson then experienced a long return fire from the Dornier. This seemed to be tracer but had no apparent effect on his Hurricane. After a third onslaught from 100 yards astern, flames sprang from the starboard mainplaine. It was clear that the Dornier was destroyed.

Both Green 1 and Green 2, P/O J B Latta, had already been singled out by a group of 8–10 Messerschmitt 109s. Green 2 engaged one and fired for 6–8 seconds—a long time in terms of aerial combat. The only evasive tactic taken by the German was a steep climbing turn left. He then instantly lit up in the cockpit, like a struck match, and spun off the climb—and continued spinnning. The fighter would not recover from such a situation.

Latta was then attacked and a bullet jammed his port aileron. He dived steeply to get a second to think. Luckily he was not followed, and he got back to base.

As Bader had gone into his own attack, Sgt R W Lonsdale in Yellow 4 saw 3 Messerschmitt 109s speeding towards the rear of 242 Squadron and about 1,000 feet below. He made a quick turn but could not catch them. Then he found himself on the tails of Dornier 215s. He attacked the rearmost one which swung across the rest. Lonsdale found he was virtually touching the tail of another Dornier, slightly to one side of it. His Hurricane was being hit by heavy cross fire from the rear gunners of the bombers, but he managed to dispose of the balance of his ammunition in to the Dornier.

While carrying out this second attack he was being hit repeatedly in the engine and the controls. Smoke began to seep into his cockpit—as well as streams of glycol mixture and oil. His controls were practically useless except for the elevator. As he broke away from the attack, the enemy had smoke wisping from the fuselage and an engine stuttered to a halt.

Lonsdale baled out at about 19,000 feet and came to earth in a pine tree at Caterham. His Hurricane took its own course down, crashing rather symbolically on Kenley aerodrome about 200 yards from the main guardroom. While dropping to ground, a Spitfire pilot flew round Lonsdale all the time to protect him till he touched down.

The time: 17.40 hours. The squadron: 310. Flt Lt G L Sinclair was Yellow Leader as he turned to attack the bombers. But he saw Messerschmitt 109s hurtling down on them from port. The squadron was turning starboard and he turned slightly port to see what the Messerschmitts were doing. Without any further warning, Sinclair received a hard blow across the shoulders. This was accompanied simultaneously by a loud noise and followed by three more distant bangs. He then found his Hurricane in an inverted spin. He was thrown hard against the roof of the cockpit. He was apparently without any starboard plane, though he found it very difficult to discern anything in that position. He had to think quickly. He decided to get out. He had much trouble in opening the roof and undoing the straps, due to the pressure in the cockpit. But he knew he had to somehow–if he were to live. At last he did it and just shot out into space without any further effort on his part.

The parachute descent took nearly 13 minutes and Sinclair landed in a wood just off the Purley Way at Coulsdon. He was picked up by Lieutenant G D Cooper of the Irish Guards from Caterham. Cooper had been watching the whole action through his field glasses and told Sinclair what had happened. F/O Boulton also flying a Hurricane had collided with Sinclair, and Boulton's machine had afterwards collided with a Dornier 215–both machines crashing in flames. Boulton was lost. Sinclair luckily survived. So a Dornier had been destroyed but at a cost of one pilot and two Hurricanes.

P/O Fejar flew as No 3 to Sinclair's section. After preliminary skirmishing, Fejar found one out of 8 Messerschmitt 110s. It tried to wriggle free by a series of twists, turns, climbs and dives, but Fejar hit it with a trio of attacks. Smoke from the port engine encouraged him to make one more attempt and the whole port side of the Messerschmitt 110 licked into fire.

But at that precise second in time 22,000 feet over south-west London, Fejar noticed the starboard leading edge fairings of his Hurricane were loosened. The fighter began to vibrate badly and head towards the ground. He slowly pulled up the nose. He reckoned that the Hurricane had been hit not by the enemy but by a splinter from an anti-aircraft shell. He left the battle and landed at a place reported as Pittesburg.

After the sight of the two Hurricanes colliding in front of him, P/O Bergman saw a Messerschmitt 110 tailing a Hurricane. He increased the boost and followed the enemy. The Hurricane broke away safely. Bergman hit the Messerschmitt 110 with a determined burst. Both engines blazed with a blackness that turned into a red glow. It was a victory for sure.

Sgt Hubacek also saw the collision. He had a brush with Heinkel 112s as variation from Dorniers and Messerschmitts. Next he found a quartet of Messerschmitt 110s and set about them from the side out of the sun. The last one retaliated but Hubacek did likewise.

The fuselage and rudder of the Messerschmitt 110 were both fragmented and he saw several splinters fall away from the machine, wafting into airspace. It was to be hoped they did not hit anyone on the ground. The enemy dived into a cloud, and counted as a probable for Hubacek, who had fought hard from 20,000 feet right down to 8,000 feet.

At 20,000 feet over East London, P/O Rypl made several turns. Above his head he saw enemy fighters not yet in action. When he saw that some of them were on to his section, flying below, he chased one. He got in a shot or two at this Messerschmitt 109 from 150 yards and saw grey smoke gushing out of one engine. His altitude at this precise stage of the proceedings read as 23,208 feet! This must take any award as the most accurate height reading made during the entire Battle of Britain!

Rypl flew on. He chased bombers, eluded fighters, and at length saw that he was over a hilly and partly wooded countryside. As he was by then flying with the reserve petrol tank open, and had therefore not much time for orientation—and as he could find no aerodrome—he decided to make an emergency landing to save the aircraft. He did his very best and landed in a long field with the undercarriage down. Unfortunately, the field was obstructed with anti-invasion-glider wire fixed on wooden poles which Rypl could not possibly see from above. So his Hurricane was damaged after all, though he was safe. The visibility by that time of the September evening had grown rather poor as well.

Back aloft the battle was approaching its latter stages. Sgt Rechka had to cope with three Messerschmitt 110s who all chose to fly for him. He gamely fired at the first one and actually hit its port engine. Diving away in distress, the Messerschmitt 110 could easily have come to grief over the suburbs south-east of London. Rechka did not see.

P/O Zimprich wanted to make a really typical Czech dash at Dornier 215s with the leader of his section but he lost his number 1 in a sharp turn. This was all too easy to do. So he tried to go for the Dornier alone. Then he saw a Messerschmitt 110 so transferred to this adversary. He scored on the port engine before having to evade other 110s seen in his mirror.

That was not the end of Zimprich's sortie. He picked up a Dornier 215 and decided to destroy it at any price. Closing from above and from starboard at 300–50 yards, he sent him spinning down. But Zimprich went round to the front and port this time from 50 yards, repeating it from starboard. He saw both engines stopped, the gunner cease firing, and the Dornier gliding. Then he espied things falling out of the aircraft, presumably bombs being jettisoned. The Dornier landed near Westerham without its undercarriage down. Zimprich circled and saw the Army approaching the Luftwaffe crew. He landed at Biggin Hill aerodrome safely.

Nine Spitfires of 19 Squadron saw the enemy initially as the Luftwaffe were flying north-west. The fighters wove and searched above the bombers. It had been arranged by Bader for 19 Squadron to take the fighters. Flt Lt W G Clouston as Blue 1 put them in line astern and clambered up to 23,000 feet, preparatory to an attack on half a dozen Messerschmitt 110s also on the climb. Just then a pair of 109s cut across their bows and Blue 1 caused one to burst before them. The second started a downward glide.

The squadron went on to tackle the Messerschmitt 110s. But Blue 1 had used all his ammunition so could not participate further. He had had his moment. Blue 2, F/Sgt H Steere, cut across in front and Blue 3, Flt Lt E Burgoyne, took a full deflection shot, closing to 50 yards before breaking away underneath. The enemy was then slipping inwards and Blue 1 saw it fade into a left-hand spiral out of control. Blue 2 chased another Messerschmitt 110 out over the Channel but failed to get in range. Blue 3 stayed with Blue 1 and so did not take part in the main attack: he preferred to protect his leader which he did successfully.

Red 1, Flt Lt W J Lawson, opened fire on the tail of a Messerschmitt 110 at 300 yards, scoring a starboard strike. With bits of wing blown off the Messerschmitt the aircraft finally crashed five miles east of Biggin Hill.

Red 2, S/Lt A G Blake, did not fire in the first dogfight but followed the main enemy formation out to sea, and stumbled on a straggling Heinkel 111. He left it dropping, flaming, towards the waterline. Red 2's windscreen was pierced by a bullet which ended in his petrol tank. Red 3 got on to a Messerschmitt 109. Some of the enemy's engine flew out in a surrealist manner and P/O W Cunningham left the 109 flame-enveloped. Red 3 got a bullet in his mainspar.

Yellow Section now. Yellow 1 attacked one of two 109s with a 150° deflection burst. No hit. He was F/O F M Brinsden and saw a Hurricane going for a Heinkel 111, so he joined in from dead astern until he could fire no more. By that time, around 18.00 hours, Red 3 had landed at Detling and the Heinkel 111 was down to 1,000 feet, with both engines stopped and his flaps and undercarriage down. He was gliding east, aiming to make a forced landing a little south of Detling, too.

Yellow 2, P/O A F Vokes, dived to attack one of six Dornier 215s, straggling and with its wheels down. He fired all he had and then left it to another Spitfire. Yellow 3, Sgt D G Cox, shot down a

Messerschmitt 109. But Cox's Spitfire was hit during the exchange in the mainplane and the airscrew. It also transpired later that he, too, had a bullet through the petrol tank. He was lucky to get away with that . . .

Douglas Bader could not see a single other British fighter in the sky by this time and maintained that the fleeing Germans could have been broken up still more severely and savagely and shot down if two fresh squadrons had arrived. The enemy adopted identical tactics as with previous interception made by 242 Squadron. They had approached from the south, flying north over the west side of London, before turning south-east for home. 12 Group Wing were instructed to patrol North Weald and Hornchurch, a useless procedure in Bader's experienced view because he could see 50–80 miles to the east but no distance to the west—up sun. In his considered opinion, quite unshaken and in fact substantiated by 9 September, they should have been patrolling many miles south-west, where they would have been up sun from the enemy and could have attacked before the Germans got to the Thames. Bader was convinced they would have shot down at least twice the number. If Sector Controllers would have confined themselves to telling formation leaders where the enemy were supposed to be and left it to them to choose height and place to patrol, much better results would have been achieved. Bader insisted with good evidence that if aerodromes like North Weald and Hornchurch wanted protection the patrol line should have been somewhere west of the Thames in the evening and south-east in the morning, because of the sun. The Battle of Britain was being fought not at ground level or some plotting table but five miles high above the Thames Estuary, London and Kent zones.

So what were the results claimed by the three-squadron Wing on 9 September? 21 enemy aircraft were destroyed, with 5 probables and 2 damaged. Our casualties were 4 aircraft destroyed or missing, 3 damaged and 2 pilots killed or missing. The individual squadron claims read as follows:— 242 Squadron, 11 destroyed, 2 probables; 310 Squadron, 4 destroyed, 2 probables, 1 damaged; 19 Squadron, 6 destroyed, 1 probable, 1 damaged.

Let us leave the postscript to 9 September once again to Johnnie Johnson:

'Fortunately for Bader neither North Weald nor Hornchurch was attacked, otherwise Park might have lodged an official complaint with Dowding, who, however, would have taken into account the tremendous results of this engagement—twenty enemy aeroplanes destroyed before bombing, for the loss of four Hurricanes and two pilots. And Leigh-Mallory must have thought a bit of occasional poaching like this was well justified, for he was so delighted with the results that he offered Bader two more squadrons, making five in all, for the next show. So it was in 12 Group, if not in 11 Group, that a leader could interpret instructions from the ground as he thought fit.'

Perhaps it was just as well that 12 Group had a breather for 24 hours. During the night of 9–10 September, few raids reached recent targets. The 12 Group headquarters accounted for this respite in two ways. Firstly, the enemy were by now still concentrating their main attack against London. Secondly, the weather became very showery in the north-west and spread diagonally across to the south-east and on to the coast of France. The bomb tally was at Wolverhampton, Manchester, Newark, Grantham, Bourne, Bircham Newton, Cambridge and Stowmarket. A solitary day raid dropped five high explosives on Yarmouth at 11.25 hours but the prevailing drizzle and dullness prevented fighters making contact.

CHAPTER 7

The Third Wing Action

This could only be England. At the height of the Battle of Britain, Her Royal Highness the Duchess of Gloucester visited 12 Group headquarters. Hitler and the Luftwaffe notwithstanding sherry was served formally in the large ante-room before lunch on Wednesday 11 September. Leigh-Mallory was there too. The Duchess left camp at about 14.10 hours.

One hour later at 15.20 a Wing took off from Duxford under the command of Sqn Ldr Lane. This comprised half of 19 and 266 Squadrons and the whole of 74 and 611 Squadrons. They had the by now familiar notice to patrol the Hornchurch/North Weald area at 23,000 feet. At least the altitude was getting more realistic. Between London and Gravesend AA fire drew their attention to an enemy force of some 150 aircraft flying generally north at 20,000 feet. The Germans were flying north in waves of tight formations of Dornier 215s, Heinkel 111s and Junkers 88s, with protecting fighters. Messerschmitt 110s were behind the bombers and a formidable force of Messerschmitt 109s behind them at about 24,000 feet. It had been arranged that the two Spitfire squadrons in the lead (composite 19/266 and 611) were to attack the fighter escort, while 74 Squadron aimed at the bombers. As 74 Squadron went for the force of Junkers 88s, they met Heinkel 113 fighters diving on them, but they gamely continued their policy of striking for the main formation. For once, Douglas Bader was not in the scrap!

Eight aircraft of 19 Squadron and six of 266 Squadron were leading the Wing. They dived in line astern for a head-on attack on the leading dozen Heinkel 111s and their screening Messerschmitt 110s. After this first attack, Red 1 Sqn Ldr B E Lane broke off to port and saw the enemy turning south-east over Sittingbourne. He went for the nearer of two 110s blowing bits off its starboard engine and then setting it alight. The other 110 opened the throttle and left. Red 1 tried for the Heinkels and saw some flames emerging jaggedly from one.

Sgt Jennings as Red 2 finished off a Heinkel, and moved on to the end one of 15 Messerschmitt 110s. It fell out of the force and crashed in a wood somewhere between Sittingbourne and Maidstone. Red 3 was Sgt H A C Roden. He took on 30 Messerschmitt 110s endeavouring to form a circle. Pieces flew from the port mainplaine of one and it took a shallow dive. Red 3 did not see what happened next as he had to take urgent evasive action himself or he might have been hit.

Flt Sgt Hawin at Red 4 knocked lumps off both engines of a Heinkel 111 from a mere 50 yards. The bomber went into a tell-tale spiral. Then a Dornier 215 decided to go for him—unlikely but true. It shattered his windscreen and registered a hit on his engine. The Spitfire was not in good shape. Hawin switched off his engine and forced landed in Kent with no drastic damage to the fighter or himself.

Green 1, F/O L A Haines, climbed to engage 40 Messerschmitt 110s slightly higher than the Heinkels. They formed a defensive circle but he penetrated to one, which he hit from 200 yards. As he was in the midst of this attack, Messerschmitt 109s swooped down on him and hit his Spitfire in both mainplanes. Haines hurriedly made for ground-level and crash-landed, both tyres being punctured during the combat. He was not hurt. Green 2, P/O Dolezal, hit a Messerschmitt 109. As he followed its belching trail, he was hit from behind and wounded in his right knee. His engine was hit too, but between them they got back to base.

Blue Section had to interrupt their main attack as Messerschmitt 109s roared up from the rear. Blue 1, F/Sgt H Steere, fired at two of them. Blue 2, Sgt D G Cox, took Messerschmitt 110s instead. Then he stopped the starboard engine of a straggling Dornier 215.

It was after 16.00 hours by now. The AA fire which had originally drawn attention to the enemy was proving troublesome and downright dangerous during the widespread mêlée. Despite hampering the plan of attack, 74 Squadron stuck to their task and inflicted considerable losses on enemy bombers. 611 Squadron went for both bombers and fighters.

611 Squadron encountered the enemy over the Thames Estuary at altitudes from 18,000–24,000 feet. The squadron was formed up in three sections of four Spitfires in line astern. At 20,000 feet their gaze was met by the rather daunting aerial spectacle of 15–30 Dornier 215s and some Heinkel 111s at 18,000 feet; a mass of Messerschmitt 110s stepped up behind at 20,000 feet; and the Messerschmitt 109s behind them at 24,000 feet. A spread of 6,000 feet. The squadron split up.

Flt Sgt H S Sadler, Yellow 4, gave a Messerschmitt 110 long

bursts from 500–100 yards, using nearly all his ammunition in his enthusiasm. The enemy fuselage caught fire and the Messerschmitt lost height.

P/O J W Lund, Blue 4, dived on to a Messerschmitt 109 and fired a short deflection burst. Another enemy hove into his mirror so he climbed, only to run into five Messerschmitt 110s. He hit the starboard one with an astern attack.

Sgt A D Burt caught a Heinkel 111 from 300 feet above it. The enemy rear gunner ceased abruptly. Other tracer fire caused Burt to invoke a steep climbing turn. The Heinkel seemed to have gone.

Sgt S A Levenson was really outclimbed by the rest of his section when they started pursuing the bombers. As he flew around 50 Junkers 88s he met a pair of Messerschmitt 109s circling in the opposite direction. Turning on to them he made a 60-degree deflection attack from the rear and allowed both aircraft to pass through his sights while he fired from 200 yards. One of them turned on its back and began to spin. Levenson lost sight of it and climbed back above the Junkers.

The bombers flew in a tight shape. He attacked the starboard line of bandits from the front quarter, allowing the whole lot to pass through his sights while firing from 100 yards. Two of them broke away below. He hit an engine of one of them and the aircraft glided down 10,000 feet in ten miles. Levenson flew actually alongside for some time until the AA guns opened up. He broke away as black smoke suddenly sooted out from underneath his instrument panel. He tried to make Kenley aerodrome but before he got near enough his engine stopped. It was a matter of skill to survive. He glided down with wheels up and brought the Spitfire to a reasonable landfall in a field not far from the aerodrome. A nearby searchlight post crew told him that the enemy aircraft he had been trailing down had crashed 6–10 miles south of Kenley. Sgt Levenson returned to his base at Digby by train on the following day!

F/O D H Watkins climbed towards the sun and at 16.15 sighted 40 Dornier 215s under AA fire. As he was about to attack them, two anti-aircraft bursts upset his Spitfire in its dive and the engine stopped. He had no option but to force land at Hornchurch and later returned to Duxford thence to Digby.

Sqn Ldr H E McComb followed by P/O T D Williams were about to take on a 110 when a 109 attacked them instead. They did not manage to locate any other enemy. Flt Lt K M Stoddart fired 1748 (!) rounds at a Messerschmitt 109 without any result. F/O Ibde Hay covered Stoddart's rear so never got within range of the Messerschmitt 109. P/O D H O'Neil and P/O D A Adams both fired at a Dornier 215 but then the AA got in their way.

Sgt F E R Shepherd and his Spitfire No 0 7298 were both missing.

The outcome of this third Wing patrol was that the 36 aircraft involved destroyed 12; with 14 probables; and 7 damaged. Our casualties were 3 aircraft destroyed and 3 damaged; 1 pilot killed and 1 wounded. The individual squadron scores were:— 74 Squadron, 6 destroyed, 3 probables, 2 damaged; 611 Squadron, 2 destroyed, 3 probables; 266 Squadron, 3 probables, 4 damaged; 19 Squadron, 4 destroyed, 5 probables, 1 damaged.

After these first three Wing patrols, Air Vice-Marshal Leigh-Mallory reported on his tactical conclusions, which are worth recording as an interim viewpoint:

1. During the first three wing formations, the following two main difficulties were experienced:

(a) The fighters who were attacking the bombers got unduly interfered with by enemy fighters. This would appear due to the fact that there were not sufficient fighters both to neutralise the enemy fighters and to attack the enemy bombers successfully.

(b) It was also found that after the Wing attack had been delivered, there were many enemy bombers who had become detached and were easy targets, but who could not be attacked because there were no fighters left with sufficient ammunition to carry on the engagement.

2. As a result, the following conclusions were arrived at:—

(a) For an operation of this type to be really successful, three objects have got to be achieved.

   i) to neutralise the enemy fighters while the attack on bombers is being made;

   ii) to break up the bomber formation;

   iii) to shoot down the bombers after (ii) has been achieved.

(b) From the size of enemy formations we have met up to the present, it was considered that at least two Spitfire Squadrons are required to neutralise the enemy fighters.

(c) In addition to the two Squadrons required to neutralise the fighters, at least three Squadrons are required to break up the enemy bomber formations and carry out the main attack on them.

(d) It was hoped that when the bomber formations had been disintegrated one of the two Squadrons neutralising the fighters might be able to detach itself and shoot down isolated bombers.

During the night of 11–12 September, the Liverpool–Crewe railway line was blocked by bombing and the Liverpool–Bala water pipeline became fractured. Before midnight other raids centred around the Humber, with later thrusts at East Anglia. The places reporting bombs were Hull, Lincoln, Grantham, Wolverhampton, St Helen's, Warrington, Digby, Ely, Mildenhall and Stoke. This gave a fair idea of the enemy's diffused intentions, diluting his energies between industrial and aerodrome targets.

By day, intermittent rain combined with poor visibility to preclude any fighter contacts, although the Luftwaffe succeeded in dropping bombs south of Wellingborough.

Many 12 Group aircrew had received awards for their flying, but no-one will mind if Douglas Bader is singled out on this day, when it was announced that he had won the Distinguished Service Order.

Again neither memorable as a night nor a day in the overall battle. Sporadic raids in the Mersey and Midlands did minor damage, while one raider dropped high explosives and incendiaries near Mildenhall aerodrome before beating a hurried exit. The daytime weather continued cloudy with occasional rain plus the extra hazard of thunder. There was literally no enemy activity in 12 Group, nor were any squadrons needed to assist 11 Group. Perhaps just as well, for this was Friday 13 September . . .

It was almost as if with a sense of impending history that the Battle of Britain resumed its upward curve on 14 September, ready for the following day. Night activity on 13–14 September registered as the smallest scale yet. One raid came in over Boston, flew over five aerodromes, and finally decided to bomb Mildenhall. Another raider beat that record by over-flying eight or more aerodromes before signifying he knew where he was by bombing the environs of Cranwell.

Thick day cloud made attempts at fighter interception hard. After midday the level of activity rose, with the main targets as East Anglian aerodromes and coastal towns. During the middle period of the day, 74 Squadron at Coltishall were very busy, since the other squadrons based at Duxford were ready and eager to participate in any Wing action that might develop—11 Group permitting! During the forenoon, 74 Squadron, Blue Section—Flt Lt J C Mungo-Park, P/O A L Ricalton and P/O R J E Boulding—chased and severely damaged a Messerschmitt 110 about ten miles north of Happisburgh, setting its starboard engine ablaze.

Then about 14.00 hours, 74 Squadron, Yellow Section sighted a Messerschmitt 110 and a Junkers 88. P/O B V Draper was the only pilot who contrived to open fire but he destroyed the Junkers. After blowing off its starboard engine, the starboard wing also dropped down in the North Sea and the Junkers crashed 40 miles south-east of Yarmouth. In addition, 74 Squadron, Red Section damaged a Heinkel 111 near Lowestoft and Green Section hit a Junkers 88 north-east of Ipswich.

Contrary to popular conception, the Big Wing of five squadrons did not fly on the offensive for the first time on 15 September. For on 14 September Douglas Bader took up the following squadrons: 242, 310, 19 and 611. They left for the London area at about 16.00 hours but made no contact with the Luftwaffe. Sgt Marek of 19 Squadron had to break away from the formation owing to oxygen trouble and his aircraft crashed killing him.

Then a couple of hours later, the Bader Wing of five squadrons took off for the first time intending to intercept. The squadrons were 242, 310, 302, 19 and 611. Five squadrons as envisaged by Bader and Leigh-Mallory. Bader was told to patrol the Debden/North Weald/Hornchurch region, but once again they failed to sight the enemy. Not their fault of course. But at least the sortie had provided practice for the next round in the Battle of Britain—a date that has gone down into human history.

11. Spitfire squadron: armourer prepares a fighter for further action, while the pilot has a word with the mechanic.

2. Air Chief Marshal Sir Hugh C T Dowding, GCVO, KCB, CMG.

CHAPTER 8

The Decisive Day

Although no-one knew it then, Sunday 15 September was the day that the Battle of Britain was won. Over the south-east of England the day dawned a little misty, but cleared by 08.00 hours to disclose light cumulus cloud at 2,000 to 3,000 feet. The extent of the cloud varied, and in places it was heavy enough to produce light local showers. But visibility remained good on the whole, with a slight westerly wind shifting to north-west as the day advanced.

The first enemy patrols arrived soon after 09.00. They were reported over the Straits of Dover, the Thames Estuary, off Harwich and between Lympne and Dungeness. At about 11.30 hours Goering launched the first wave of the morning attack, consisting of 100 or more aircraft, soon followed by 150 more. These crossed the English Coast at three main points, near Ramsgate, between Dover and Folkestone and a mile or two north of Dungeness. Their goal: London.

This formidable force comprised Dornier 17s and 215s escorted by Messerschmitt 109s. They flew at various heights between 15,000 and 26,000 feet. From the ground the German aircraft looked like black dots at the head of long streamers of white vapour; from the air, like specks rapidly growing. They appeared first as model aeroplanes and then as the range closed, as full-size aircraft. One controller said: 'This looks like the biggest show yet.'

Battle was soon joined, and raged for about three-quarters of an hour over east Kent and London. Some one hundred bombers burst through our defences and reached the eastern and southern quarters of the capital. A number of them were intercepted above the centre of the city itself, just as Big Ben was striking the hour of noon.

To understand the nature of the combat, it must be remembered that the aircraft engaged in it were flying at a speed of between 300 and 400 miles an hour often. At that speed, place names became almost meaningless. The enemy, for example, might have been intercepted over Maidstone, but not destroyed on the return route until within a few miles of Calais.

'Place attack was delivered–Hammersmith to Dungeness.'

'Place attack was delivered–London to the French Coast.'

These phrases in the reports forcibly illustrate the size of the area over which the battle was being fought. In fact it took place roughly in a cuboid about 8 miles long, 38 miles broad, and from 5–6 miles high. It was in this space between noon and half past twelve that 150–200 individual combats were waged. Many of these developed into stern chases only broken off within a mile or two of the French coast.

Sixteen squadrons of No 11 Group followed by five from No 12 Group, took off to engage the enemy. No 10 Group was also utilised. All but one of these squadrons in the battle came face to face with the Luftwaffe very soon after taking to the sky. Five squadrons of Spitfires opened their attack against the oncoming hordes over the Maidstone/Canterbury/Dover/Dungeness area. These were in in action slightly before the Hurricane squadrons, which intercepted further back, between Maidstone, Tunbridge Wells and South London.

The Few found the enemy flying in various types of formations. The bombers were usually some thousands of feet below the fighters, but sometimes this position was reversed. The bombers flew either in Vics of from 5–7 aircraft, or in lines of 5 aircraft abreast, or in a diamond pattern. The Messerschmitt 109s were usually in Vics. One pilot saw the enemy as attacking in little groups of nine, arranged in threes like a sergeant's stripes. Each group of nine was supported by nine Messerschmitt 110 fighters with single-seat Messerschmitt 109s or Heinkel 113s circling high above.

The enemy soon realised that our defence was awake and active, for the German pilots could be heard calling out to each other over their wireless planes:

'Achtung! Schpitfeur.'

While Spitfires and Hurricanes were in action over Kent, other Hurricanes were dealing with those of the enemy which had broken through to the London outskirts by sheer strength of numbers. Fourteen squadrons of Hurricanes, almost at once reinforced by three more of Spitfires, took up this challenge, all of them coming into action between noon and 12.20. Then followed an engagement extending all the way from London to the coast–and beyond.

It was precisely 11.22 hours when 242 Squadron were ordered off from Coltishall. The Wing comprised 242, 310 and 302 in that order, plus 19 and 611 Spitfires. The five squadrons formed up according to plan over Duxford and at once proceeded south towards the action. For once they had been scrambled in time. They were speeding to the Luftwaffe at height, at the very time the enemy were over the Channel. The Wing sped south to patrol a flexible area beyond the Thames in the Gravesend region. Bader made sure he had the sun behind them as 242, 310 and 302 reached angels two five, with 19 and 611 stepped up behind them to an altitude varying between 26,000 and 27,000 feet. The Hurricanes had the task of harrying the bombers, while the Spitfires kept fighters at bay. So much for the theory. The practice was about to begin.

Douglas saw two squadrons passing right underneath them in formation, flying north-west in purposeful manner. The enemy looked like Dornier 17s and Junkers 88s. AA bursts caused Bader to turn the Wing. He saw the enemy again now 3,000 feet below. He managed to perfect the approach with 19 and 611 Squadrons between the Hurricanes and the sun. The enemy were still below and down-sun. Next he noticed Messerschmitt 109s diving out of the sun, so he warned the Spitfires to look out for the Messerschmitts and also to watch for friendly fighters. The Messerschmitt 109s broke away and climbed south-east.

Bader was about to attack the bombers which were turning left to west and south when he noticed Spitfires and Hurricanes of 11 Group presumably already engaging them. He was compelled to wait in case of a collision. Then he dived down with his leading section in formation on to the last section of three bombers. 'Leader calling—prepare to break—line astern.'

As P/O N N Campbell took the left-hand Dornier 17, Bader went for the middle one while Sub Lt R J Cork took the right-hand—which had lost ground, or air, on the outside of their turn. Bader opened fire at 100 yards in a steep dive and saw a sudden large flash behind the starboard motor of the Dornier as its wing caught fire. The shots must have hit its petrol pipe or tank. Bader overshot and pulled up steeply. Then he carried on to attack another Dornier 17 but had to break away to avoid an oncoming Spitfire. The sky seemed full of both Spitfires and Hurricanes queueing up. They were metaphorically pushing and jostling each other out of the way to get at the Dorniers, which were for once really outnumbered. Bader squirted at odd Dorniers from close range as they silhouetted into his sights, but he could not hold them there for long still for fear of collision with the friendly fighters. Bader was flying as Red 1. He saw a collision between a Spitfire and a Dornier 17 which wrecked both aeroplanes instantaneously. He finally ran out of ammunition while chasing a crippled and smoking Dornier 17 into clouds. Bader realised even in the midst of the mêlée that there for the first time really the 12 Group Wing had position, height and numbers.

This is an extract from how Douglas Bader himself described those minutes around 12.15 hours somewhere over Hammersmith:

'At one time you could see planes all over the place, and the sky seemed full of parachutes. It was sudden death that morning, for our fighters shot them to blazes.

'One unfortunate German rear-gunner baled out of the Dornier 17, I attacked, but his parachute caught on the tail. There he was swinging helplessly, with the aircraft swooping and diving and staggering all over the sky, being pulled about by the man hanging by his parachute from the tail. That bomber went crashing into the Thames Estuary, with the swinging gunner still there.

'About the same time, one of my boys saw a similar thing in another Dornier, though this time the gunner who tried to bale out had his parachute caught in the hood before it opened. Our pilot saw the other two members of the crew crawl up and struggle to set him free. He was swinging from his packed parachute until they pushed him clear. Then they jumped off after him, and their plane went into the water with a terrific smack.

'I've always thought it was a pretty stout effort on the part of those two Huns who refused to leave their pal fastened to the doomed aircraft.'

But Bader was only the leader of 56 aircraft. What happened to the other 55? We left Sub Lt R J Cork nosing for the starboard Dornier 17 of the rear section. After the first sally, he dived to the right, climbed again, and saw the starboard engine of the bomber groaning and flaming. The Dornier did a steep diving turn to port and down. It was now also being fired on by four other Hurricanes and a Spitfire, so Cork decided not to pursue. Instead he fired at another bomber, in company with a trio of other friendly fighters. It was last seen steeply falling into the clouds and must have failed to recover. Cork contributed a completely unsolicited testimonial to the Wing Leader: 'The success of the whole attack was definitely due to the good positioning and perfect timing of the C.O. of 242 Squadron, who was leading the Wing formation.' So even if Douglas did not account for more than one definite Dornier plus other damaged, the final figures soon to emerge would be because of his shrewd skill.

P/O N N Campbell was Bader's Red 3, as he attacked a Dornier 17 from astern and below. The lower gun of the bomber fired close to his Hurricane, but ceased soon after Campbell fired back. Smoke billowed and blew from the lower part of the enemy fuselage, so he could claim one Dornier damaged.

Successful as this engagement was, the element of risk remained present for the RAF just as for the Luftwaffe. Yellow 1, Flt Lt G E Ball poured all his fire towards a Dornier 17 without noticeable result. But then he sustained a hit in his own fuel tank. The Hurricane caught fire quickly but Ball managed to lose height while still in control and bring down the fighter in a field a few miles from Detling. Yellow 2 was P/O N K Stansfield. During an astern attack on another Dornier 17 the rear gunner fired at him steadily. But Stansfield silenced the enemy which dived for cloud protection with smoke streaming in ragged parallels from both engines. He followed it through the clouds to make sure of the outcome. The Dornier crashed directly on top of a house, but Stansfield had no time to wonder about either the Germans or the occupants of the house.

Blue 1 was to have an adventurous day, only he did not know it yet. Flt Lt G S Powell-Sheddon made several stabs at Dornier 17s, some in company with other Hurricanes. While setting an engine on fire at one stage he nearly collided with a Hurricane also after the same bomber. Three of the enemy aircrew baled out as the Dornier descended and crashed into a small wood near a house. The bomber exploded on impact and the whole tree area appeared enveloped in a single sheet of flame. Powell-Sheddon landed at Duxford to find he had a bullet hole through his oil tank. But the afternoon was still to come . . .

Meanwhile behind Blue 1 came P/O Tamblyn as Blue 2. He fired on a Dornier 17 at 150 yards and turned away till friendly fighters had completed their attacks. He remembered Bader's advice about watching out for our own fighters. Next time at the Dornier 17, he noticed slight smoke from the enemy engines which decreased a little. But the damage had been inflicted in company with five other friendly fighters. They followed the Dornier down to 2,000 feet when the crew baled out. The bomber crashed near West Malling in a field. Tamblyn thought one of the crew failed to survive. Blue 3, P/O J B Latta, for once could make no definite claims though he did engage the enemy more than once.

On to Green Section now. Green 1 was P/O P S Turner who chose a straggling Dornier to attack three times at 100, 100 and 50 yards respectively. The last close-range pressure hit home and burst the oil tanks of the doomed Dornier. Three crew managed to get out before it began its final unpiloted plunge into the inevitable field, where it blew up. Turner thought there seemed to be an inexorable acceptance of their fate on the part of the Germans from the moment his Hurricane opened up. Turner told his number two: 'Close up Green 2—I'm going in now.' Sgt E Richardson as Green 2 was not lucky in his attacks but he survived.

The last of the trio in this section was P/O Hart at Green 3. Seeing that the enemy bombers were well engaged and on equal terms, Hart veered to go for the next nearest thing—a Messerschmitt 109. It was flying at 15,000 feet in the general direction of France. Hart proceeded to dive on him from behind and above, forcing the enemy down to 11,000 feet. This put the Messerschmitt right on top of the cloud layer which had built up a little since early morning. Hart continued his gentle dive on the enemy till he was directly above it. Then he instigated a steep dive and opened fire at 150 yards. Hart's bullets completely smashed the pilot's enclosure and the engine cowling. Flames spurted. Hart flew on after him through the clouds, overshot him, and saw the Messerschmitt 109 disturb the surface of the Channel some 8 miles off the English Coast. Hart then patrolled up and down searching for any stragglers but saw nothing further.

All the 242 Squadron managed to get back to Duxford except Ball, but at least they had lost no pilots. Would the other four squadrons fare so well? How many men would survive this day? These questions still remained to be resolved.

Flt Lt J Jeffries was leading B Flight of 310 Squadron when they saw the enemy first. The Luftwaffe were west of London and flying north, but as the Wing turned south to attack the enemy also took a turn southward. Jeffries led B Flight on the inside of the turn until they were abreast of the leading squadron. They dived on the enemy and he fastened his sights on one particular machine. He caused its port engine to catch fire, whereupon it was taken over by some other Hurricanes. That was a Dornier 215. Jeffries attacked another 215 and its occupants baled out almost at once. He did the same thing again and a second Dornier crew also baled out. A Spitfire then dived straight through the fuselage of this Dornier and the fighter went down out of control.

P/Sgt Kominek started an attack with the leader of his section, Flt Lt Jeffries, but at 15,000 feet he lost sight of him. Probably because the flight lieutenant was four miles above Kingston on Thames while Kominek had by then reached Tunbridge Wells! He and three Hurricanes fought a Dornier 215 which made the clouds. The other Hurricanes went elsewhere but Kominek persevered with three more bursts. After the last one from 200 yards, some sheets started to fall off the bomber and smoke signals appeared. The crew just dumped their bombs over the Kent countryside and baled out not far behind them. The Dornier ploughed into an already furrowed field three miles south-west of Tunbridge Wells. One Dornier 215 to the credit of Kominek.

P/Sgt Kaucky shared a Dornier 215. He delivered his effort over London at 12.05–12.10 hours from 100 yards or so. Two other

Hurricanes were also in the fight. Kaucky used up all his ammunition and between the three Hurricanes they saw the Dornier 215 going groundwards—minus its crew.

At about the same time and place, P/Sgt Hubacek had an exchange of fire with a Dornier 215. Hubacek was making his run from the port and the rear, and the enemy soon started to glide. Another Hurricane helped in the conflict. The enemy glide steepened to a dive as several more Hurricanes and Spitfires joined in to seal the agony of the enemy bomber. At 8,000 feet part of the rudder of the Dornier 215 broke off altogether. Two men got out. One did not. The Dornier crashed somewhere south of London. As Bader said: it was sudden death this morning.

Finally in 310 Squadron, Sgt Puda of Green Section challenged a pair of Dornier 215s. At an angle of 20 degrees he opened fire from 100–150 yards. The aim must have been impeccable for the bomber fell with both engines streaming. Puda broke away left to prepare for a further finishing-off. But just then a Spitfire did it for him from 50 yards.

The Poles followed the Czechs. P/O J Chalupa leading Green Section Flight B of 302 Squadron saw the bombers through puffs of our anti-aircraft fire. He got in three bursts at the leader of the second vic in an enemy Dornier squadron. The range was shortened dramatically from 250–30 yards. The bomber dived violently. After breaking into a left turn, Chalupa saw a second Dornier 17. He attacked three-quarters from above and slightly to port getting in two 3-second bursts at 100 yards. Smoke and flames from the port engine signified success. Two airmen jumped out of the burning bomber which dived to earth. Meanwhile one of the other Polish pilots cut off the tail of this burning aircraft with his own wing—tearing it in the process.

The Poles were certainly going in irrespective of survival. Flt Lt Chlopik at Red 1 Flight A went for the hindmost section of Dorniers, doing a beam attack from port. He hit a Dornier 215 and saw its port engine smoking heavily, with blue smoke also emitting from starboard. The Dornier dived on its back to the ground. The three crew jumped out in time and three parachutes brought them down.

Chlopik was over south-east London now. He hit a Dornier 17 from behind and above. With its port engine faltering, the bomber became the focus for a whole group of Hurricanes and a couple of Spitfires. The sun was on his beam during his first fight and later behind him. Flt Lt Chlopik was flying at 14,000–17,000 feet over the southern suburbs of London. He had taken off at 11.25 from Duxford.

The report ended with the poignant words: 'This pilot could not sign as he was killed . . .'

The Poles knew what freedom meant—and the lack of it. They were willing to risk everything in their passionate nature to try to restore it to Europe. Bader will not forget Chlopik. Nor should we.

302 Squadron had height advantage as they flew their Hurricanes in at 300 mph. F/O Czerwinski in Blue 2 Flight B met a Dornier 17 above and in front of him. He went in alone with three bursts. The port engine sparked into fire and the Dornier dived. Three other Hurricanes also attacked this Dornier 17, so that by the time Czerwinski had gone in again the bomber was written off by the crew, who had wisely jumped.

Flt Lt Jastrzebski at Red 2 Flight A flew down sun, gave a Dornier three or four brief squirts and paused to consider the situation. His first burst from height and side started at 300 yards and ended at 50 yards. The Dornier did not fire back but wiggled sharply to left and then right. Another Hurricane went for it, too. Red 2 turned 180° to the right of the Dornier and did not see it again. But on climbing he saw 5 parachutists. Owing to loss of position he landed at Henlow and refuelled before returning to Duxford. Jastrzebski shared the Dornier 17 with Chlopik, so they must both have been attacking the same machine.

F/O Kowalski at Red 3 Flight A fired at the last Dornier of a group from 80 yards. Two bursts of two seconds each. The bomber took to the clouds, but Kowalski was sure it must have crashed. Below the clouds he saw two more Dorniers already being set on effectively by our Hurricanes. After a few seconds, both enemy bombers plummeted.

F/O J Palak in Green Section Flight B was one of three Hurricanes sharing a Dornier 215. It crashed. Palak climbed again with a right-hand turn to notice a more formidable and perhaps worthier opponent—a Messerschmitt 109. It was diving towards another Hurricane at that instant, so Palak turned towards him at full throttle, squirting twice. Bits spun off the Messerschmitt as it took a vertical dive. Palak could only claim a probable, although the aspect of the enemy machine made it unlikely that any recovery would be possible. Palak landed at Maidstone at 12.35 hours.

Also in Green Section Flight B, Sgt Paterek encountered enemy bombers probably Heinkel 111s flying in formation of five close together at a measured speed of 270 mph. He made a beam attack. The enemy rear gunner of the bomber selected ceased to reply. That left Paterek free to aim a long burst at very short range. He could scarcely miss and the bomber took the inevitable course downward out of any semblance of control. There was no smoke. The altitude at the start of the dive was 5,000 feet. It never recovered and fell the remaining mile to earth. Paterek was not exactly familiar with England yet and landed at the likeliest-looking aerodrome he could find. It turned out to be Wattisham—from where I flew my first Lightning a quarter of a century later!

Sqn Ldr W Satchell was actually leading 302 Squadron. As Douglas Bader had headed for the most westerly of the three formations of enemy bombers, Satchell took the middle group, flying in vics. He attacked the left leader and saw him go down straight. In this attack Satchell followed Bader's advice and dived from above the enemy almost vertically, giving a full deflection shot which seemed effective. He went through with the dive before pulling up. This strategy presents a fairly easy shot and does not give much of an aiming mark for any enemy gunners. But Satchell did in fact get scratches from a few stray bullets. His Hurricane got the scratches, not himself. Then as he commenced to attack another Dornier he was hit by a Messerschmitt 109 but survived. Then he spotted a dozen Dorniers east of London flying east-south-east. Satchell made a beam and quarter attack from either side and saw one of them falling. It might have landed between Rochester and the coast.

Blue 3 was Sgt Wedzik who got on the tail of a Dornier 17 on the port side of its group. At the end of his firing burst, he observed the bomber in dire distress. Smoke from the port engine, flames from the port mainplane. The bomber banked steeply to the left. He did not see the end of it, as he returned over London trying to find his leader. But being unable to do so, headed back to Duxford. One hour and ten minutes after take-off.

Last in the Polish squadron was Sgt Sindak at Yellow 2 Flight A. He paced a Dornier 17 at 240 mph before squirting at it. The usual black smoke, this time from the cockpit and port mainplane. The enemy rear gunners fired at him spiritedly. Sindak lost the machine-gun panel of his port mainplane, while the whole mainplane looked to be badly torn. The Dornier spun down, as a second Hurricane finished it off. A large piece flew off the underbelly of the fuselage. 302 Squadron had done well.

So to the two Spitfire squadrons ranged higher than the original 25,000 feet of the Hurricanes. Flt Lt Lawson led 19 Squadron as they spotted a score of Dornier 17s escorted by Messerschmitt 109s. The enemy were 10,000 feet lower down. He hurried on ahead of the enemy bombers and turned to deliver frontal fire. He dived past the left-hand Dornier 17 of the rear vic of the enemy. Then he turned and attacked the same aircraft from its rear—300 down to 50 yards. Fragments fell from the starboard wing. The starboard engine started streaming glycol. The enemy 'waffled' away from the rest and glided down with glycol still streaming out. The result: one probable, Dornier 17.

'Tally ho! Tally ho! Bandits ahead and below me.' The air rang with such typical pilot jargon. The RAF might be utilising hunting vocabulary. The quarry was human and in the present state of history more justifiable than fox-hunting.

Sqn Ldr Lane, Sub Lt Blake and P/O W Cunningham were flying in one section of Flight A. Cunningham as No 3 attacked behind the other two but did not really get a chance to fire. Veering off on a solo, he fired at a solitary Messerschmitt 110. Its starboard engine was hit and stuttered after this attack which closed in to 50 yards. Cunningham turned in from the port to deliver another squirt from that side. The Messerschmitt 110 was already as good as done for—when a pair of Hurricanes shot it from the sky. The three of them had shared this success at angels 16.

F/Sgt Unwin was Red 3 to Flt Lawson's Red 1, Flight A. The bombers were in vics of three as their escorts dived singly on Red Section. Unwin took on a Messerschmitt 109 with a yellow nose. This was at 20,000 feet over Westerham—shades of Winston Churchill. The six-second burst proved enough and the German fighter pilot baled out. His Messerschmitt actually came down between Redhill and Westerham—around the Surrey-Kent border country.

Behind Red 3 came F/Sgt H Steere as Red 4. He too saw the 109s bearing on them and so broke to port to close. He fired one burst from a poor position, then chose a better angle to attack another. His first deflection fire from 350 yards soon diminished to 50 yards. As near as safety allowed. Thick bluish smoke swirled around the Messerschmitt 109 as it spiralled into the clouds. The steepness of the near-vertical fall signified destruction. Steere chased another Messerschmitt 109, came into range, only to find that he had no ammunition left—so no point in hanging about longer. Take-off time had been 11.30 hours. He landed at 12.40.

Green 1 Flight B now. He was F/O L A Haines. South of London near Biggin Hill he gave a good deflection burst at a Messerschmitt 109. It half-rolled and dived to 12,000 feet but then straightened out again. Haines was flying faster than the 109 and had to pull away rapidly right to avoid a collision. The Messerschmitt 109 really rolled. Smoke seemed to be pouring from underneath the pilot's seat. He went down with it to 6,000 feet and had to be careful to recover from this drastic dive, as the enemy was by then touching 480 mph. Haines made his way more slowly through a bundle of low cloud and as he emerged he saw the wreckage of the Messerschmitt already burning on the ground. It had been painted yellow from spinner to cockpit. Haines climbed through clouds and narrowly missed hitting a Junkers 88. This bomber was actually on fire and was being pounded by numerous other Hurricanes.

The locale: Tunbridge Wells. The height: 15,000 feet. Green 3 Flight B, Sgt D G Cox, had one or two abortive brushes before finding a Messerschmitt 109 about to attack him head-on. As the enemy passed above Cox, the Spitfire pilot turned and climbed steeply. He came up underneath the 109 with a couple of bursts, stalling as he did so. The next time Cox saw the fighter was when it had begun a flat glide that steadily steepened. It hit earth five miles east of Crowborough.

Bader's five squadrons were working. The second Spitfire squadron was 611. Red 1 Flight A saw the bombers at an estimated 18,000 feet with their screening Messerschmitts at 28,000 feet. But Bader's perspicacity had put the Spitfires almost up to them. Red 1 was 5,000 feet above and to one side of the main wing Hurricanes. They were flying north-west with the sun more or less on their left. As the Wing went into the attack, the 611 Spitfires kept company with 30 Messerschmitt 109s who were further west and slightly higher. They did not descend. After the Wing had broken up, the bombers turned round through 180 degrees to south-east. Red 1 waited for 5–7 minutes before he told Bader he was coming down.

Red 1: 'Echelon port.' They were then going south-east, still up-sun of both the Wing and the enemy.

They made a head-on ramrod thrust on to ten Dornier 215s and 17s. Red 1 took a Dornier 215 head-on. Next a Messerschmitt 110. It turned over on its back and went down in a death-throe. Red 2 behind him could not follow. Red 1 tried to pick up any enemy lame ducks along the coast but saw none.

611 Squadron attacked in three sections of four Spitfires in line astern: Red, Yellow and Blue. Yellow 1 Flight A was around angels 18 as he sped some ten miles west of Canterbury. He first tried a trio of Dornier 215s. Then he picked out a single Dornier 215 and fired all he had at this one. Its port engine literally exploded. Red 2 saw the crew bale out. Other Spitfires seemed to be going for this same unfortunate Dornier but Yellow 1 got the credit and it crashed 7–10 miles south-east of Canterbury.

Yellow 2 Flight A was in the same area really: a moving triangle that at the time of his main action was pinpointed by London/Rochester/Herne Bay. Rochester with its memories of Dickens and *Great Expectations* and the marshes. Another century. Another world.

'Bandits at angels 18.' Yellow 2 heard the phrase and acted on it. He dived on 30 Dorniers from about 4,000 feet above them. No luck. Next he chased a Dornier 215 towards Rochester. The Dornier 215's altitude began to dwindle as it neared the Herne Bay zone. Smoke from port engine. Crew baled out. The Dornier crashed on the edge of a wood or thicket some four or five miles south of Herne Bay. It burst into flames. Four attacks had to be completed before this final chalk-up. Yellow 2 himself was not exactly unscathed or fully fuelled. He landed at Detling, owning up to being slightly lost by 13.00 hours.

Last of the morning's sections in this mammoth Wing action was Blue Section 611 Squadron. Blue 4 caught a Dornier 215 by itself at 14,000 feet. Blue 4 rolled over and carried out an old astern attack by diving on to the bomber. One long burst and both enemy motors began to smoke. Blue 4 climbed and carried out the same drill again. By this time, though, the Dornier had both its engines obscured by smoke and fire. Also fire tongued from both main-planes behind the engines. The result: one more Dornier destroyed.

There was scarcely time for a snack, let alone to add up the morning's score. But this was what the Bader Wing had been credited with in a little over an hour. Fifty-six fighters had destroyed 26 enemy aircraft; with 8 probables; and 2 damaged. These were the individual squadron scores as listed by 12 Group on that midday. 242 Squadron, 5 Dornier 17s and 1 Messerschmitt 109; 310 Squadron, 4 Dornier 215s; 302 Squadron, 6 Dornier 17s and 2 Dornier 215s; 19 Squadron, 3 Messerschmitt 109s and 2 Messerschmitt 110s; 611 Squadron, 3 Dornier 215s. Twenty-six enemy aircraft.

13. Czech fighter squadron: when the pilot lands in his Hawker Hurricane, the squadron mascot is there to meet him.

14. Formation of five Heinkel 111s with Junkers Jumo engines.

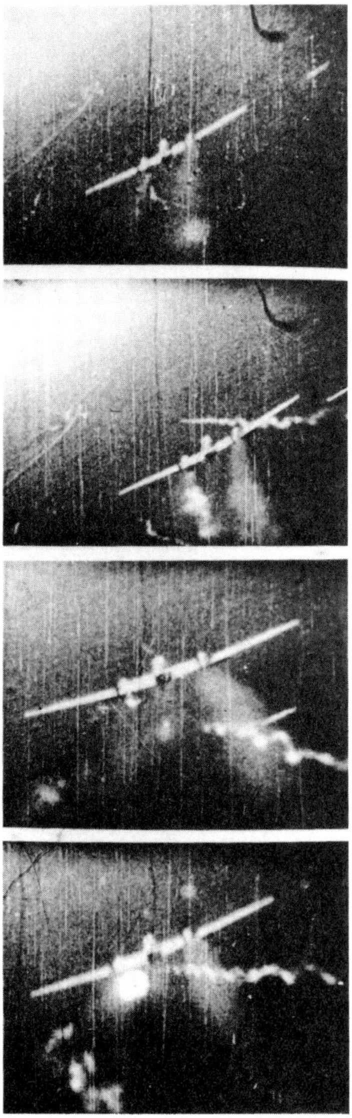

End of a Messerschmitt. The enemy tries to escape, leaving twin trails of exhaust smoke. But then hits on the port engine cause it to burst into flame.

16. Pilot's eye view: RAF combat film taken during the Battle of Britain gives intimation of speed of aerial combat. These frames show view of Me 110 at moment of attack and just afterwards—with smoke pouring from it.

CHAPTER 9

The Climax Comes

Hardly had the Wing landed and refuelled when they were ordered up again—and again vindicated the strategy conceived by Leigh-Mallory and Douglas Bader.

The take-off time: 14.12 hours.

The clouds were eight-tenths at 5,000 feet. The Wing consisted of 49 fighters instead of the 56 in the morning/midday combat. But the same five squadrons were involved. Bader led them up through a gap in the clouds and hurried south still climbing. The three Hurricane squadrons—242, 310, 302—were in line astern and the pair of Spitfire squadrons on the right. The three Hurricane formations climbed slightly more quickly of the two types of fighter. Douglas and 242 Squadron were at 16,000 feet and still rising when they sighted quantities of enemy bombers punctuated by the dark burst of anti-aircraft shells. The enemy were at 20,000 feet, still three or four thousand feet higher. This was just the sort of situation that tended to annoy Bader. Those precious extra minutes or warning to get airborne might have enabled them to gain the additional altitude so that they could have been plus 4,000 feet instead of minus it. Bader endeavoured to climb and catch the enemy, but 242 were set on by Messerschmitt 109s from above and behind. Douglas told the Spitfires to come on and get the bombers, while he and his fellow Hurricane pilots broke up and engaged the enemy fighters. Bader was nothing if not decisive. Then things started to happen all over that particular patch of sky between the Kenley/Maidstone ground area.

After ordering the break up, Bader himself pulled up and around violently. Coming off his back, he partially blacked out and actually almost collided with Yellow 2, P/O Denis Crowley-Milling. That could have been the end of a glorious friendship. Bader spun off Yellow 2's slipstream and straightened out at only 5,000 feet. He had not fired a shot yet. However, he climbed back into the fray and got in a brief burst at a twin-engined bomber flying westwards. He was just in the enemy's range and fired a three-second squirt from a completely stalled position. He then had to spin off again and lost still more height. Eventually he went through the clouds near Ashford, Kent, to try and trace any enemy stragglers but it was no use. Bader was furious at the whole situation. They were all too low. They had to seize whatever opportunities they could. He had to admit that his lead was not as effective as it could have been in better circumstances. They were up-sun, too low, and he spun out of position. He turned his mind once more to the inescapable truth: if they had managed to get off 10 minutes earlier and reached their height, then the whole story could have been better. That was the perfectionist thinking of course. The reality of the situation was rather different, at least in that the Wing did manage to do phenomenally well given their abysmal location.

Douglas did not mind missing his personal victories on this occasion and was naturally pleased later to hear how well things had gone after all. The faithful Sub Lt R J Cork as Red 2, to Douglas in Red 1, made height at the maximum speed. As soon as Douglas told them to break formation, Cork went sharply to the right accompanied by a Messerschmitt 109. He was now in a dive and suddenly found himself flying right through the second squadron, thereby losing his quarry in the process. But he spotted a Dornier 17 to the starboard aiming north-westwards.

Cork dived 6,000 feet into the attack and concentrated a prolonged squirt at its port engine which started to smoke. His next thrust was a beam one, large lumps of the Dornier tracing crazy angles in the sky as they tumbled away. The starboard wing also flushed with fire near its tip. The Dornier dived gallantly for cloud cover but Cork waited till it emerged, as it inevitably had to do. Then he simply put in a head-on assault and the Dornier 17 died. Cork climbed a thousand feet and was attacked by a vicious pair of yellow-nosed Messerschmitt 109s from above. Rather like twin insects. He did a steep tilt to the left and actually got on the tail of one. But in the middle of a promising burst of firing he ran out of ammunition. The other fighter was then on his tail, so he put his stick into a virtually-vertical dive down to 2,000 feet and got away unscathed. Red 3, Campbell, fired a couple of thousand rounds at divers enemy but made no claims.

Yellow Section got up to 21,000 feet: nearer the height that Douglas would have preferred. Yellow 1, P/O N K Standfield, saw a Heinkel 111 flying below cloud and under attack from two other Hurricanes. Yellow 1's burst stopped the enemy port motor and by then both engines were in dire trouble. So the Heinkel was too.

Other aircraft also fired on this rather unfortunate Heinkel which eventually pancaked on to an aerodrome south-east of London. The aircraft carried a crew of five. On its tailplane were painted three pinkish stripes presumably to imitate similar markings being painted on RAF aircraft and so confuse any attackers.

Denis Crowley-Milling as Yellow 2, having survived the near-miss with Douglas Bader, picked out a Messerschmitt 109. This particular enemy fighter performed a whole series of barrel rolls and aileron turns before he finally hit it. No amount of writhing seemed to make any difference. The machine caught fire around the pilot's cockpit and Crowley-Milling followed it down according to instructions–seeing it crash several miles south of Maidstone. While the midday battle had been over London, this afternoon's encounter moved south-east into central Kent. Yellow 3 was P/O N Hart, who engaged the enemy but modestly refused to make any claims.

The time was around 15.00 hours now. Three-quarters of an hour and more since the slick take-off. Flight B Blue 1 was Bader's friend Powell-Sheddon. He reported 200 enemy aircraft. One other pilot had put it more succinctly: 'The whole bloody Luftwaffe!' Powell-Sheddon was in action from London towards the South Coast from 15.00 hours.

He saw swarms of 109s mostly higher than 242 Squadron, plus hordes of bombers. All approaching London. Two hundred plus. Messerschmitt 109s flashed out of the sun and from behind. One came head-on and he fired at it. Then he saw some 30 bombers flying north-west for the capital who were *not* being attacked by any of our fighters–from 11 or 12 Group. Blue 1 broke away from the dog fight after them. He passed under several Messerschmitt 109s who left him unmolested. Before he caught up with them, the bombers had turned round and were heading SSE.

Flt Lt Powell-Sheddon got between them and the sun–and 1,000 feet above. He picked off a Dornier 17 flying a few spans away from the rest and fired. Heavy smoke and fire followed his second and third attacks. All his attacks came from the sun and slight beam. After his last effort, he climbed back into position and saw the Dornier disappear into 7/10ths cloud in a tight spiral with volumes of smoke as signals of impending impact. He assumed the Dornier would crash somewhere near Rye.

Powell-Sheddon set off for Duxford in a gradual dive for low cloud at low speed to economise his dwindling fuel. Almost at once he was pounced on by a Messerschmitt 109 which must have scored a crucial hit on his Hurricane which became uncontrollable. Powell-Sheddon felt shaken up and baled out. He landed safely though his left arm felt temporarily paralysed. The reason was that he had dislocated it. He was soon in Rye Hospital, and credited with one Dornier 17 destroyed.

The afternoon was turning into a slightly more golden tone. The time: 15.15. P/O P S Turner in Blue 2 sent a 109 into an uncontrollable spin. He could not be sure that it crashed but he did believe the pilot was dead—hence the lack of attempt to correct the spin. He could not cogitate about it for long.

A shell gun cartridge exploded in the side of his Hurricane under its tail and hurled Turner into a spin. He retained consciousness however, and recovered control. He found he was below the clouds. The sortie went on. He attacked a Dornier 215 from a beam using full deflection. The bomber's starboard engine smouldered and the Dornier took a gentle dive. It hit the ground and exploded between some houses near a river bank east of Hornchurch. None of the crew of the wrecked bomber got out.

P/O J B Latta was another old chum of Bader. Flying Flight B Blue 3, he was under attack from Messerschmitt 109s. One of them overshot him so that he was able to get in a burst from 50-75 yards dead astern. The fighter was still on fire as it entered cloud at 5,000 feet. Latta was over the Maidstone zone at this phase and he could not visualise any recovery for the damaged Messerschmitt, which was really right out of control.

As now usual, 310 Squadron followed in Douglas and 242. Flt Lt Jeffries was leading the squadron of Hurricanes when they sighted the black-bomber blocks above and ahead. Then 310 was jumped on by Messerschmitt 109s and the Wing as such broke up. Jeffries was in Flight B and rose rapidly to 24,000 feet into the sun as planned. The enemy fighters turned west. Jeffries decided to wait till they had done this manoeuvre to aim a head-on attack at them with the sun behind him. He started, continued his dive straight through their first formation. They were east of London. He fired at number three of the leading Messerschmitt 109 section, whose starboard engine caught alight. It broke away in anguish and went down.

Behind Jeffries came in Sgt J Rechka in Blue Section. He and two other Hurricanes took a Heinkel 111 so utterly that following it down Rechka saw the Heinkel 111 crash-land on the beach near Foulness. He saw two of the crew get out and recorded the fact impassively. This bomber was credited as shared with Sgt Prchal and another Hurricane.

Same flight, different section. P/Sgt Jan Kaucky of Green Section was in the vicinity at the equivalent battle time of 14.40–14.50–15.00. He and two Spitfires from another unidentified squadron shot down a Dornier 215. All three RAF aircraft had more or less met at the Dornier, and Kaucky fired one short accurate burst. The Dornier fell through clouds with yet more fighters after it, and it eventually met its inexorable end. Kaucky meanwhile was following another bomber as far as the coastline, where it vanished into cloud. At that stage he felt it pointless to continue out to sea, so turned round and headed for home.

Over with A Flight, its leader was Sqn Ldr Hess. But P/O Fejfar was close behind him in the same section as a bevy of Messerschmitt 109s joined battle. Nothing conclusive results. Next, Hess and Fejfar plus three other Hurricanes and a pair of Spitfires encountered a dozen Dornier 17s. The last section of enemy bombers were dispersed. One aircraft attacked by Fejfar had a stream of what was probably petrol colouring its wake. Fejfar went back for the Dornier 17s. As one went in and out of cloud, the 310 pilot fired at him twice with results that took scant time to realise. The Dornier dropped though still in some degree of control. Fejfar followed it down to see it make an emergency landing near the Isle of Grain. He flew over it until he was sure that civilians had approached it and taken the crew prisoners. A satisfactory sortie for him and 310 Squadron, so he nosed back for Duxford. The Czechs had done well once more.

The day had yet to take final toll of Allied airmen. Seven of the Polish 302 Squadron were told to scramble at 14.10 hours and gain Angels Twenty as soon as humanly possible. The instructions were to fly due south where enemy aircraft of over a hundred strong were about to cross the coast of Dover.

'Will you patrol Canterbury?' The controller Woodhall had 'asked' Bader. The rest was up to him. 302 Squadron were the rear of the trio of Hurricane formations. When the drones of Dorniers dotted into view, Messerschmitt 109s were circling around above them like birds of prey: which they were. Blue 1 veered to go for fifteen enemy aiming east. Just before getting into position, Blue 1, Sqn Ldr W Satchell, spied a Messerschmitt 109 in his mirror, flying above him. He waited until the Messerschmitt dived to attack and then pulled up sharply letting it pass below him. Blue 1 then got on its tail and pressed several long bursts. The Messerschmitt 109 groaned on to its back with smoke issuing—and spun to the Kentish ground.

Seeing that Blue 1 was busy, Blue 2, P/O Pilch, dived for the bombers. He found that Red 1 had also done the same thing. The enemy formation fanned out for cloud cover, so Blue 2 waited underneath until they emerged. Then he took a Dornier 17 from above and head-on, noticing that no fire came from the German gunner. At the same second, a Spitfire attacked this Dornier too.

Blue 2 made a double-quick turn and attacked from it tail, getting in a trio of bursts down to almost zero feet. The smoke signalled hits and the downward direction signified the rest. From some 6,000 feet the Dornier turned towards the Thames Estuary losing height the worse it burned.

Just then, Blue 2 saw a Dornier 215 taking a peep out of the tea-time clouds. He saw the rear-gunner take aim and fire briefly—but after Blue 2's response there was nothing more seen or heard. Smoke had started from the Dornier's port engine but the usual end was interrupted by heavy AA fire bursting all around the Hurricane. He waited impatiently for it to stop and went in for the kill. The Dornier dived into the shallow waters not far off Margate.

Blue 3, P/O Kaiwowski, prepared an attack at about this moment but as he did so his port machine-gun panel became loose. It did not fly off completely, but caused very strong drag and prevented proper control of the Hurricane. Blue 3 was probably uttering Polish curses by then, but he had no choice but to dive away and find a field safe for landing. His left undercarriage wheel got in a rut and broke away, the fighter finally coming to rest with a broken undercarriage. But the pilot was safe. Blue 4 also had the misfortune to be forced to break off his intended attack owing to engine failure. He eventually got back to Duxford all in one piece—pilot and plane. He was F/O Czerwinski.

Red Section 302 Squadron had a tragic time. Red 1, Flt Lt Chlopik, was actually attacking enemy Dorniers before Blue 2 arrived on the scene. He caused one to break up. Flt Lt Chlopik later was forced to bale out during a particularly violent exchange with the Luftwaffe and for some reason unknown was not able to pull his parachute ripcord. He was killed.

Red 2, P/O Lapka, dived for a Dornier 17 from the beam. At this moment his starboard machine gun panel blew up, causing a heavy drag. Lapka was hit by fire from the Dornier 17 rear gunner and smoke filled his cockpit. Then at an altitude of 15,000 feet he dived away and things looked bad for him. But after a few frantic instants —as many pilots have experienced at some stage in their combat careers—he managed to bale out, pull the cord, and sail to earth. His total damage was a minor foot injury.

Red 3, F/O Kowalski, found a lone Dornier 17. The Pole took a steep left turn and swooped down on it from above and behind. He did not open fire till he was within 30 yards of the bomber. He could actually discern the small lettering on the Dornier's tail flank. The tailplane disintegrated and considerable chunks of wing also careered from the bomber. It dived at 45 degrees for the ground.

Red 3 then saw another Dornier ahead of him. He noticed its rear gunner calmly firing tracer at him. He chased the enemy, got in a good burst from 100 yards and watched the start of its fall. He got in another burst at its belly as it fell. Red 3 had nothing left to fire with so flew after the Dornier at 20 yards' distance, seeing it steadily, progressively, dive out of all control. On landing, Red 3 found that his flap and undercarriage were not working properly and one of his wheels was punctured.

So to the Spitfires. Sqn Ldr B J E Lane was leading 19 Squadron. Simultaneous to seeing 30 Dornier 215s, he glimpsed higher up the fighter escort screen at about 30,000 feet. Three Messerschmitt 109s dived on Lane and his men. Lane lunged to starboard and a loose dog-fight ensued, with more Messerschmitt 109s coming down. Lane could not get near to any of the immediate enemy aircraft, so climbed to take on a collection of Messerschmitt 110s. No result, though.

Suddenly his second sight became aware of a couple of Messerschmitt 109s just above him. He manoeuvred around on the tail of one and fired. The Messerschmitt 109 seemed a determined type and took positive and violent evasive action. While screeching for cloud cover, the Messerschmitt 109 received a burst of five seconds from Lane. The enemy flicked over, inverted, and entered a cloud doing a shallow inverted dive. It was to all intents and purposes beyond pilot control.

Lane left it and flew south to grapple with two further formations each of some 30 Dornier 215s. They did not appear to like his head-on attack and jumped about while he was passing through their ranks. Despite their discomfiture, Lane could claim no victory from this phase, but at least his Messerschmitt 109 seemed more than probable.

Lane was Red 1. Flt Sgt C H Unwin at Red 3 also saw the German bombers in vics of three line astern. Above there seemed to Unwin to be 'thousands of Messerschmitt 109s'. He was somewhere over Kent, at Angels Twenty-Five Plus. He engaged a Messerschmitt 109 at close range, which half-rolled as it dived into the clouds. Unwin followed keenly but during the descent amid the cloud his windscreen froze up at 6,000 feet and he lost sight of the Messerschmitt.

Clambering back to 25,000 feet, Unwin saw a pair of Messerschmitt 109s passing over his head flying south-south-east. He chased them and caught them at Lydd. He shot down the first, which went into earth, beach or water near the coastline—he could not say for sure just where it fell. The second attack was equally devastating. Unwin's firing seemed accurate, for the other Messerschmitt 109 took a vertical thrust waterwards and ended up just off the Kent coast.

Flt Lt W G Clouston of Flight B took both Blue and Green Sections into an assault on Dornier 17s. He set the starboard engine of one afire, followed it into clouds, and saw it in a gap. The altitude at that stage was lowering from 10,000 to 6,000 feet. Clouston made a beam attack as the Dornier emerged from cover. Some ten feet of the bomber's port wing snapped off. Their particular fragment of the fight was going on off the coast between Southend and Burnham on Crouch. One of the Germans baled out over a convoy 15 miles east of Burnham. Clouston continued pressing home his attack on the depleted plane until it went down towards the sea, rolling over and over to port. The Dornier 17 had been destroyed definitely. As Clouston had by then used all his ammunition anyway he headed for the Essex coast which he reached after flying for nine minutes at about 260 mph. So he reckoned he had been some 30 miles out to sea.

Behind Blue 1 came Flt Sgt H Steere as Blue 2. Steere followed Clouston towards the Dornier 17s and singled out one on the right. He closed from 350 to 50 yards, firing most of the time. Chunks and lumps flew off the Dornier, whose port engine caught fire. The crew baled out and then the bomber 'waffled' into the clouds. Three bombs had been jettisoned before the crew had abandoned the Dornier—and in fact they dropped uncomfortably close to P/O Vokes bringing up the rear of this particular party piece.

Vokes was Green 2. He saw one German, then another, bale out of the stricken Dornier after Steere had hit it. Vokes climbed back into the fray and was surprised by a Messerschmitt 110 sneaking in from astern. Tracer fire flashed past the starboard wing of the Spitfire, one bullet passing through the main spar. Vokes climbed steeply and after two or three minutes of aerial ballet finished on its tail. Vokes 'gave him everything I had' closing from 200 to 50 yards. The starboard engine of the enemy was really streaming. If the aircraft had been human, it would have been bleeding badly. It seemed out of control as it hit the clouds. What could be worse than being in an uncontrollable aeroplane diving vertically through blinding clouds? Equally awful for German or British alike.

F/O L A Haines was Green 1 in Vokes' section and estimated the enemy forces at two hundred. He had already claimed a Messerschmitt 109 at midday. Now at 14.40 hours over the Thames Estuary he noticed a quintet of Messerschmitt 109s forming a defensive ring. One rolled off so Haines peeled off too. At 15,000 feet the enemy flattened out. Haines took remorseless aim as he closed to 50 yards. The Messerschmitt lasted only a matter of a few more seconds.

Haines reclimbed to 25,000 feet and patrolled the coast near

Beachy Head. After a quiet five minutes he saw a lot of bombers being attacked by Hurricanes. The bombers were escorted by numerous Messerschmitt 110s which circled on sighting the Spitfire. Haines waited a little longer, closed on a couple, fired at one, and scored a direct hit on the starboard motor.

Haines was on the receiving end of fire now, so decided to use up all his ammunition quickly. The enemy was diving badly. Haines noticed the rear gun draped along the fuselage. Bits were being hurled from the Messerschmitt 110 as it fell. Haines was the persevering type of pilot and followed it to the bitter end. The Messerschmitt just managed to scrape through the air till it got to the French coast, where it crashed on the beach. Haines scampered for home!

Flt Lt W J Lawson led Yellow Section. P/O W Cunningham flew at Yellow 3. They were attacked from behind by Messerschmitt 109s. Sgt Roden was hit. Cunningham broke off to try and help. After a dog-fight with a Messerschmitt 109, he lost the main party but saw three Messerschmitt 109s speeding east. With a Hurricane for moral support, he attacked this trio. Yellow 3 took the left hand machine, closing to 50 yards. The attack was made through the altitude belt of 16,000–14,000 feet. The other Messerschmitt 109 dived for cloud cover at 11,000–9,000 feet. Cunningham saw his Messerschmitt 109 reeling ablaze into the clouds and claimed its destruction. He reckoned reasonably that it would have gone down somewhere towards the Dover area.

Red 1 leading 611 Squadron ran into groups of bombers before gaining enough height. They ignored these targets as they rose westward to keep the Messerschmitt 109s off the Wing. There were only eight Spitfires in 611 and they could not outclimb the Messerschmitt 109s in time.

As 25 Dornier 17s seemed to be flying south unmolested, and the squadron had got away from the Wing anyway, Red 1 ordered sections 'Echelon Right' and they dived. Red 1 took the rear Dornier. The rear gunner stopped firing and it seemed all over in moments. Smoke from port engine. Red 1 pulled up into a loop and dived in an inverted position. By then the Dornier was on the descent leaving a smoky flame wake. Red 1 blacked out badly in the clouds but his victory was confirmed by Yellow 2.

Red 2 was P/O Williams and he found a Heinkel 111. But to his surprise if not chagrin a five-second burst from 80 yards did not hit it. In fact the enemy had the temerity to be firing back! Williams was then at 18,000 feet to the south of London when he saw a score of Dornier 215s flying west. They turned north but his particular Dornier 215 went left and lost height. Williams attacked again, followed it into clouds and was only 100 yards astern as he observed one of its engines stopped. He did a slight right-hand gliding turn in the cloud, then 2,000 feet thick. Below the haze he could not see the aircraft but did spot one enemy airman dropping by parachute. The German landed safely on the edge of a wood near Hawkhurst Golf Club some five or six miles north of Hastings—near where another battle had been waged a mere 874 years earlier on!

Flt Lt Heather followed Red 1 into the attack and chose a stern attempt on 20–30 Dornier 17s. He took the machine next to Red 1's as his adversary was already aflame. He fired every single round of his ammunition at one Dornier and as he broke away it bore all the evidence of numerous hits. Messerschmitt 110s then swooped on Heather, Yellow 1, but he swerved clear. The claim was one Dornier 17 destroyed. Yellow 1 took off from Duxford at 14.15 hours but landed at Croydon at 15.40.

Yellow 2, P/O Brown, followed Red 1's attack on the Dornier 215 which had put an engine out of action. But Brown had flown rather close to the scene of this activity and oil or glycol from the enemy aircraft spattered the intervening airspace and covered up his windscreen. He had to break off as the fluid oozed down the screen. But he was not finished with the fight. He caught a turning straggler and fired a deflection burst. The enemy spiralled and though Brown tried to trace its course the dive proved too steep for safety. He noticed that the escape hatch above the pilot's seat was hanging and flapping open, due either to his firing or the crew escaping. He did not see anyone bale out, but this could have been because a swarm of Messerschmitt 109s darkened a segment of sky and Brown decided it prudent to become scarce in the clouds. The aircraft he shot down was a Heinkel 111K.

P/O Lund took on 25 Dornier 215s. But especially one 'drop-out'. One burst of fire from 45° astern was followed by another from directly above. Flashes of fire. But three or four other Spitfires were also after this Dornier, so the damage could have been caused by them. Lund climbed to 19,000 feet. He was deterred by the presence of six Messerschmitt 110s—not nice odds. One of these was coming at him anyway, so he fired a brief burst head-on and then turned. The Messerschmitt 110 flashed by on Lund's port side. He saw a smoke trail from an engine and Lund's own starboard wing was punctured by at least one bullet hole.

The extent of the battle can be gauged by the towns quoted. Having fruitlessly attacked a Messerschmitt 109 and a crippled Dornier 215, Blue 3 found himself approaching Brooklands Aerodrome at 10,000 feet. Dorniers and Messerschmitts flew above him —all after the aerodrome as a prime target. Blue 3 climbed with the sun behind him until he was 1,000 feet beneath them and 1,000 yards to the port and front. He opened fire and saw his stuff hitting the leading aircraft. The effect was that the leading vic of four broke away to port with white smoke in parallel lines from engines 1 and 2. Before the incident closed, Blue 3 glimpsed the banking of the old motor race track surrounding the aerodrome. Bader too had happy memories of those distant pre-war days and the countryside not far from Brooklands.

Flt Lt H Sadler made two attacks at least on a Dornier 215 over the London zone from 18,000 feet. A Hurricane also attacked the Dornier from line astern after Sadler had finished. Although Sadler did not actually see the Dornier go down, it was behaving in a very disabled manner, eventually fading below cloud at a mere 3,000 feet. Not a height from which to recover and return to the Continent. Sadler simply claimed it as sharing destruction of a Dornier 215. The time was 14.45–14.50 hours. The clash was nearly over. By teatime the Battle of Britian was won.

During that afternoon, the Bader Wing of 49 aircraft had destroyed a further 26 enemy aircraft, with 8 probables and 1 damaged. These were the individual squadron scores as listed by 12 Group:— 242 Squadron, 2 Messerschmitt 109s, 2 Dornier 17s, 1 Dornier 215, 1 Heinkel 111; 310 Squadron, 1 Messerschmitt 109, 1 Dornier 17, 2 Heinkel 111s; 302 Squadron, 2 Dornier 17s, 1 Dornier 215; 19 Squadron, 5 Messerschmitt 109s, 2 Dornier 17s, 1 Messerschmitt 110, 1 Heinkel 111; 611 Squadron, 2 Dornier 17s, 2 Dornier 215s.

But whereas the Wing had virtually no losses in the earlier sortie, the first signs showed RAF losses as follows:— aircraft destroyed 3, aircraft damaged 2; pilots killed or missing 2, wounded 3.

Yet summarising the claimed successes of the Bader Wing during these two sorties, the remarkable results achieved showed that for an average of about 52 fighters (56 and 49 respectively), they had destroyed 52 enemy aircraft. An average of one enemy per fighter flying.

Air Vice-Marshal T Leigh-Mallory wrote the following report of 15 September just one day later:

'Fourth Wing Patrol:

'In view of the conclusions reached, the Wing consisted of five squadrons with 56 aircraft, and took off from Duxford before noon on the 15th September. The three Hurricane Squadrons patrolled at 25,000 feet with the two Spitfire Squadrons about 2,000 feet above them. They saw about 30 enemy bombers (Dorniers) south of the Estuary flying north-west with a large number of Messerschmitt

109s protecting them. The leader saw Spitfires and Hurricanes, belonging to No 11 Group, engage the enemy and waited to avoid any risk of collision. As the Hurricane Squadrons went in to attack the bombers, Messerschmitt 109s dived towards them out of the sun, but, as the Spitfires turned to attack them, the enemy fighters broke away and climbed towards the south-east, making no further effort to protect their own bombers, who were actually endeavouring to escape towards the west and the south. They did not all, however, manage to save their skins in their precipitous flight, as the Spitfires were able to destroy a number of them before they got away. In the meantime the Hurricanes were able to destroy all the Dorniers that they could see and one of the Squadrons saw a further small formation of Dorniers, which had no doubt broken away from the main formation in the first attack, and promptly destroyed the lot. One of the Spitfire Squadrons, seeing that the enemy fighters were getting out of range, also came down and took part in the destruction of the enemy bombers. In this engagement, the prearranged idea worked perfectly, for there were sufficient numbers of Spitfires to attack the enemy fighters and prevent them from exercising their primary function of protecting their own bombers, which were destroyed by the three Hurricane Squadrons at their leisure. The enemy were outnumbered in the action and appeared in the circumstances to be quite helpless.

'Fifth Wing Patrol:

'The same five squadrons which had taken part in the Fourth Patrol, though with the slightly reduced number of 49 aircraft, took off again in the afternoon at about 14.30 hours. They climbed up through a gap in the clouds, which was 8/10ths at 5,000 feet, the three Hurricane Squadrons in line astern with the two Spitfire Squadrons to the right and slightly above them. They saw AA fire and then a large number of enemy aircraft at 20,000 feet. The leader of the Wing found that he was at a technical disadvantage as he had not had time to reach his patrol height, with the result that this formation was attacked by Messerschmitt 109s, as they were trying to get in position. Because of this, the leader of the Wing told the Spitfires to attack the bombers, and the Hurricanes to break up and engage the fighters. The results of the engagement were satisfactory so far as they went, but under the circumstances it was impossible to break up the bomber formation and so achieve the same tactical superiority as in the Fourth Patrol.'

T Leigh-Mallory

Nevertheless the five Wing Patrols to date between 7 September and 15 September had notched up the following formidable figures against the Luftwaffe, claims made immediately after the actual battle:—

Enemy aircraft destroyed	105
Enemy aircraft probables	40
Enemy aircraft damaged	18

So over one hundred enemy aircraft were claimed for the RAF losses of:—

Pilots killed or missing	6
Pilots only wounded	5
RAF aircraft lost	14

Bader with some of the Canadian pilots of his 242 Squadron.

Flt Lt G E Ball was one of Bader's right-hand men in the Canadian 242 Squadron.

19. Douglas Bader with his Hurricane. At this stage he was a squadron leader and had already won the DSO.

20. Decorations for gallantry and devotion to duty: left to right, P/O W L M McKnight, awarded the DFC, and Sqn Ldr D R S Bader and Flt Lt G E Ball, awarded the DSO and DFC respectively.

CHAPTER 10

The Battle is Won

After slight activity involving bombs on Liverpool and Manchester, as well as mid-Wales, at 07.45 hours next morning a Wing was ordered to patrol Debden–North Weald area. They consisted of 310, 302 and 19 Squadrons but made no contact with the enemy. At 08.45 they were relieved by the other two Squadrons 242 and 611. They in turn were told to land about 09.15 hours, having failed to make any sort of sightings.

During the day a fair amount of enemy fluttering was felt over the East Coast area generally with bombs in such specific places as Grimsby, Watton, Stalham and Cromer. Reconnaissance flights over the North Sea also prevailed, but showers prevented any interceptions. However while patrolling Convoy Pilot off Spurn Head, Blue Section 616 Squadron saw a lone Junkers 88. They gave chase and the enemy dived practically to sea level. Then Sgt Iverson lost touch with the other two pilots and in the gloom actually landed in the sea near a minesweeper—having run right out of petrol! He was finally landed by MTB and got back safely to Coltishall.

Heavy wind and rain in the night of 16–17 September meant merely scattered bombing in the Midlands and Liverpool. By daylight some bombs were dropped near Mildenhall aerodrome, south and west of Warrington, and in the Speke area. The last group did not strike Speke aerodrome but did hit private houses. The Wing consisting of the usual five squadrons were once more ordered or asked to patrol North Weald but they saw none of the Luftwaffe. So the Bader Wing had a two-day respite. Then came 18 September. The Battle of Britain was not yet over. Like some symphonies whose climacteric is reached towards the end of the fourth movement, this fight may have hit its zenith on 15 September but the graph and the aerial decibels had some way to go before the final bars.

The Bader Wing was despatched twice to patrol the North Weald airspace on 18 September, once at 09.00 and then again at 12.50

hours. But on neither occasion did they glimpse the Germans. Then came the third take-off: at 16.16 hours. 12 Group Wing of 242, 310 and 302 Squadrons of Hurricanes, with 19 and 611 Squadrons of Spitfires above and behind, started to patrol the zone from the centre of London to Thameshaven. Their height was 24,000 feet. At 20,000 feet the cloud reading was 10/10ths, with a lower layer at 6,000 feet, 8/10ths upper. The higher layer was spreading from the south. This top layer was only about 100 feet thick so Douglas Bader decided it was no good patrolling above it and chose instead immediately below at 19,000–20,000 feet. Suddenly he saw AA bursts to the south-west, coming eerily through the clouds, so he proceeded north-west and found two enemy groups. There were about 20–30 in each and seemed to be entirely unescorted. Flying along at 15,000–17,000 feet the Germans were approaching the first bend of the Thames, west of the Estuary, near Gravesend. The enemy were actually south of the river when Bader went for them.

242 Squadron attacked in a dive from east to west, turning north on to the enemy. Conditions seemed rather favourable to the Wing, with their targets set against the white cloud base. Never one to try and hide his few errors, Bader insisted he rather misjudged the lead-in, owing to a desire to get at them before they crossed the river. As a result, he had to resort to diving into the middle to break them up. He fired in the dive, a quarter attack turning astern at the leading three enemy aircraft—Junkers 88s. His bullets scored on the left-hand one of the leading section and as Bader arrived right in amongst them this Junkers swung away in a leftish dive, its port engine hit. It zoomed down and out of the fight towards the north bank of the Estuary, somewhere west of Thameshaven. Sgt Brimble as Yellow 3 confirmed the crash.

Bader's initial dive broke up the front of the formation and he found himself shortly afterwards among another hostile group. He gave a couple of quick squirts and then got out of this collection. He nearly collided with two of the enemy before extricating himself—and also at least one other Hurricane. He spun off someone's slipstream and lost about 3,000 feet altitude in next to no time. Regaining control, he set for the south-east. Douglas discovered a Dornier 17 rather detached so he closed to shortest range and fired. The immediate result startled him. He got no return fire but the rear gunner at once baled out and in so doing wrapped his parachute around the tailplane of the bomber. The Dornier started doing aerobatics in the shape of steep dives followed by zooms on to its back—and then repeating the process. It was losing height as Bader watched.

After the second or third performance two members of the crew baled out from in front and the Dornier was left doing its aerobatics alone with the rear gunner. Bader tried to kill him to put him out of his misery, but he was unsuccessful. The last Bader saw of this aircraft was in a vertical dive into cloud at 4,000–6,000 feet, where he decided to leave it. Bader thought it crashed either into the Estuary or south of it, not far from Sheerness.

The faithful P/O Willie McKnight was Bader's Red 2. South-east of Hornchurch about the 17,000 feet line, he scored a direct blow on a Dornier 17. The starboard engine blazed and the surest guide to the degree of damage was, as usual, that the crew baled out. McKnight plus a Spitfire found a Junkers 88 and left it without either engine running. Not the best way to try and fly. But the crew again baled out and McKnight actually saw the pilot land in a field a little north of the Thames. The bomber also crashed north of the river.

P/O N N Campbell, Red 3, followed 1 and 2 on the German group. Campbell overshot his target but then drew off to the left and sought a fresh one. A Junkers 88 had got left behind on the turn so he positioned himself astern and to the left of this bomber. Campbell could hardly miss. A short burst. Short range. The Junkers fell out of the sky.

Finding himself near the enemy again, he tried another attack. No result. After flying across the top enemy group, he found another Junkers 88 ahead of him. It had previously been fired on by a Spitfire but at the time Campbell struck it showed no visible proof of damage. Both engines gave up after short-range bullet wounds.

By this time, the sky was spreadeagled with friend and foe. Some of the enemy were still grouped but well ahead of him. At full throttle, he set out to overtake them. From below and behind, Campbell overtook slowly. When he got in range he opened fire. He damaged a Junkers 88, but at this precise second he was caught in a nasty bout of crossfire from the enemy. One machine-gun bullet hit his port mainplane. As his position was not advantageous, he broke off. Later he saw a Spitfire cause wisps of smoke to gasp out of a Junkers' starboard engine. Red 3 went in and hit the other engine, so the Junkers 88 fell with flames issuing from both.

Yellow Section followed Red. Flt Lt G E Ball was Yellow 1 of Flight A. The time was then shortly before 17.15 hours and the general area 10 miles south of London. Ball saw the Junkers 88s in a box formation and also the Dornier 17s. But no fighters. Ball followed Bader into a diving astern attack and only effected a very short burst—though the idea of breaking up the enemy box seemed to have worked. Ball broke away, gained height, and turned into a favourable position as the altimeter rose. He saw a Junkers 88 on its own and went for it from dead astern. He opened up at 300 yards and then at about 100 yards he was suddenly covered in oil. Breaking away he was naturally alarmed, but saw the starboard engine of the Junkers afire. At the time Ball thought he must have collected a bullet in his oil tank, but on landing at Gravesend as quickly as he could, he discovered that the oil had come from the Junkers, as his own oil tank was quite undamaged.

Yellow 2 engaged the enemy without much luck. Sgt G W Brimble was at Yellow 3. After seeing Bader's Junkers 88 go down, Brimble found a Dornier 17 out of its rightful place in the box. He gave it four bursts of three seconds each and finally saw it go down to earth a little north of the Thames. Brimble was still eager for action and climbed again, but nothing else seemed to be in sight. Brimble reported seeing what he could only describe as 'wire netting' being jettisoned from the Dornier he had been attacking.

F/O P S Turner must have muttered some curses as engine trouble with his Hurricane forced him to turn back to Duxford before sighting the enemy at all. Just one of those things.

He was Blue 1. P/O Tamblyn at Blue 2 found himself right in the midst of the enemy formation he had attacked! He shot at a Dornier 17 before turning to get out of his slight predicament. He did not notice any outcome of the firing, but Willie McKnight did. The Dornier was last seen by Red 2 going down in flames. One Dornier destroyed by a pilot who did not know he had done so.

Completing the Blues, P/O N Hart at Blue 3 opened at a Junkers 88 from 75 yards. He eased back on his control column and could clearly see the bits cascading off the pilot's enclosure. Hart pulled up to make another attack. This time it came from above and slightly behind. As he flew in, he saw smoke from the enclosure. He gave another short burst causing the pilot's enclosure to catch alight. The bomber dived down with all its crew. Hart followed it till the crash came on the north side of the Thames some 50 yards from a railway line. Leaving that scene, Hart turned south to see another Junkers also southbound at only 5,000 feet. Very low. He 'pulled the plug' and saw that the enemy port motor was dead, though otherwise it was all right. Hart stole up underneath it in a vertical climb, firing about 30 yards in front and hitting the wings and fuselage. The other motor gave out. The Junkers rolled over and crashed down the mile to earth.

Green Leader Flight B was Sub Lt R E Gardner, already a veteran. During his first attack he could not get in a steady burst as they dived across the enemy. At the second attempt, he found a few stragglers and made a good quarter attack on one. Port wing and motor aflame, this Dornier 17 dived steeply to its doom somewhere in the Thames Estuary—graveyard of so many bombers.

Turning in pursuit of a section of 6 or 8 bombers heading for France, Gardner caught them up after a chase lasting three minutes or more. One was flying 100 yards behind the rest, so he fired at its port engine. The propeller slowed to a halt and black smoke signalled the hit. He pulled away and then went for the starboard side. Its second engine also gave the fatal smoke signal. The Dornier glided down from about 10,000 feet over Canvey Island. Another short encounter and Green 1's ammunition was exhausted. Douglas Bader confirmed the destruction of his first Dornier, and though the other one probably went down too it could not be claimed as more than that.

P/O Bush at Green 2 followed Gardner into the onslaught on the rear of the twelve bombers. He got in a shot at one of them, causing it to drop astern apparently out of control. But he did not see any more as he was set on by a Spitfire! The Spit did not actually fire at the Hurricane but would not get off his tail. A slight case of mistaken identity—very easy in the stratified emotions several miles over the Home Counties with cloud and evening both coming up fast. P/O Denis Crowley-Milling, at Green 3, for once could not claim any successes.

Flt Lt Jeffries was leading the Czechs. 310 Squadron saw 15 Dornier 215s over London at about 19,000 feet. He drew level with them but they turned towards him, so he had to break away to avoid passing too close. Jeffries hit both engines of a Dornier 215 which went down. Sgt Kominek behind him saw it crash. The leader then followed the bombers out along the south bank of the Thames, attacking all the way. Fierce AA fire forced him to stop at one stage. As the enemy passed over the Kent coast, the Dornier he had just been firing at seemed to have engine trouble and Jeffries was doubtful if it would have reached France.

Behind Jeffries as Blue 1 flew P/O Zimprich at Blue 3. After a skirmish he found a Dornier 215 and attacked from the starboard and then the port sides. For good measure he came up from below, too. Heavy smoke obscured much of the enemy. Zimprich was already well out over the sea, near North Foreland. The Dornier glided seawards and Zimprich fervently wanted to finish it off. But his ammunition was expended so he never actually saw the bomber in contact with the sea. Claim: one probable.

P/O S Janouch was leading Red Section of A Flight. They were south of London at the 20,000 feet mark. An over-sharp turn brought them too close to the enemy on the first run-in. Next time, after they had gained height for a fresh attack, Janouch went in with two other Hurricanes. Their target was a section of Dornier 215s. Two attacks on a Dornier with a pair of Hurricanes and he saw the crew bale out. No doubt about that one. A Dornier could not be expected to find its own way back to base.

P/O Fejfar was Red 2. He was sharing the early attacks with Janouch. As one bomber started doing aerobatics, the reason became clear. The crew had left it. There was a strange visual sense about an aeroplane in its death throes with no human beings aboard.

P/Sgt Jirovdek at Red 3 got to the rear of a Dornier 215 and chalked up three separate bursts from 100 yards. Both engines were hit and the bomber was in direst distress. Two other Hurricanes hit it as well, and P/Sgt Puda actually saw it crash and 'burn down' on the ground. Till there seemed nothing left of it all. Jirovdek could claim a share of the Dornier. Sgt Puda of Green Section shared the bomber, too, and saw at least one of its crew bale out. From an angled turn the Dornier dived and crashed not far from Stanford-le-Hope.

P/O E Fechtner fired a burst at a Dornier 215 from 800 yards! He later hit it and followed it relentlessly into and through the clouds. Over the Thames Estuary he fired again and one of his bullets found the bomber's port petrol tank. Both engines ended on fire. Before the final moments the enemy gunner fired at his Hurricane and made a hole in a blade of the airscrew. Fechtner later found he had four bullet holes in his aircraft, the one in the propeller plus three in the elevator. But he was unhurt.

P/O Bergman was leader of Yellow Section, the last one in 310 Squadron. He attacked the whole lot of the Dornier 215s. Then he took one especially. He fired all his ammunition at it from 100 yards or so. The usual story with the usual end. One engine. Both engines. One Dornier destroyed. There was no more to say, nor to do.

P/Sgt Prchal at Yellow 3 fired five bursts at the bombers from 400 yards closing. In the first, one Dornier was hit, with the petrol tank eventually catching fire and sending it down. Prchal did not leave it like that. He fired again and again till the crew baled out and the aircraft spun and drilled into the ground near Stanford-le-Hope.

There was still time for some courtesy left, even amid this battle. An enemy pilot baled out. A Czech pilot reported: 'It is a matter of regret that his parachute did not open . . . '

The Poles had a field day that afternoon. Ordered to scramble at 16.50, the instruction issued came over as 'Patrol Hornchurch Angels Twenty'. 302 was the third of the two of Hurricane squadrons as usual, with the Spitfires on flank above. Thirty-plus bombers were flying north-west in vics of five. Red 1, Sqn Ldr Satchell made attacks from above before the enemy lost height. He closed to 80 yards and got in a series of shots from astern. His target bomber was enveloped by a mixture of smoke and flame and was never seen again. Before breaking away, Red 1 had his perspex covered with oil from the burning aircraft, showing just how near he was. Red 1 saw two enemy crash, one in the sea off Sheerness, the other on the peninsula between the Medway and the Thames.

Red 2, Wg Cdr Mumler, chose a different bomber on the port side. He fired but then had to break away to make room for another aircraft attacking. As he did so, he saw flames from the turret of the enemy rear gunner. Red 3, F/O Kowalski went for one Dornier, then another. At his last burst, he saw a full-size parachute open from the rear gunner's turret. It became entangled in the mainplane. Bits of the enemy aircraft flew off the mainplane from the rear, causing Red 3 to break off the combat temporarily. He never saw what happened to the unfortunate rear gunner.

Yellow Section went in behind Red. Flt Lt Farmer at Yellow 1 went for a Dornier 215 and then chased a Junkers 88. Pieces peeled off the Junkers 88 before it vanished into a cloud, by which time Farmer had used all his ammunition. Yellow 2, Flt Lt Laguna, had trouble in that he could not focus his sights properly and rather than risk hitting another Hurricane, he could do little but fly along for the ride. Sgt Wedzik was at Yellow 3. With another Hurricane, he chased a Junkers 88 out to sea, forcing it down to a dangerous altitude of only 1,000 feet. He and the other Hurricane attacked it alternately, with pieces flaking off it regularly.

P/O Pilch was leading Green Section, which caused a good break-up of an enemy group. Green 1 went right for the middle—Bader like—and saw metal careering about the sky. Next he found a Junkers 88, whose rear upper gunner fired at him the whole time while he was making five attacks on it. By the fourth attack, the port engine was obviously out of action. At the fifth attack, the enemy bomber fired a red light, clearly a signal. One man at least jumped out of the fated Junkers.

Sgt Peterek was Green 2. He also had a Junkers 88 as target from 100 yards. With one engine afire, the Junkers was attacked again from the beam and slightly astern. The crew of three called it a day and jumped—their parachutes all opening at once. But as they did so, too, a few fragments of the Junkers flew off and hit Green 2's propeller, causing the Hurricane to flutter violently. Something hit his radiator and his reserve petrol tank broke, spattering him with petrol. Green 2 wisely switched off his engine at once and glided southwards. He saw the enemy crash and then made a forced-landing himself, sustaining no further damage. Green 2 was P/O

Karwowski. He twice attacked a large group. No luck. Then he did a burst from beam and a bomber dived into the sea 'very violently'. One parachute emerged before it did so.

Blue Section went in from above and to starboard with the rest of the Poles. Flt Lt Riley as Blue 1 put paid to a Junkers 88. Both engines gave out and large chunks of fuselage began to drop off it, too. It dived away doomed. Blue 1 used the rest of his ammunition at another Junkers and saw two things: a stab of flame from the port side of the fuselage and pieces spinning off it. The bomber dived away. Another victim.

Blue 2, Flt Lt Jastrzebski, had a shot at several enemy. One dived sharply as if struck. He transferred his attentions to yet another and hit it, also noticing that seven bombers were hurrying in formation across the Channel for France to lick their heavy wounds. Perhaps seven out of a dozen?

P/O Wapniarek at Blue 3 was attacking for a second time, he saw that out of the Junkers jumped the rear gunner, near Southend-on-Sea. He wondered momentarily what would happen to the man. Blue 3 caught another Junkers 88 about to be dimmed by cloud. The bomber fired at Blue 3 from two or three guns using tracer bullets. Blue 3 was not deterred and used all his own ammunition on it. The enemy broke up completely on striking the sea. Blue 3 flew for eight minutes over the water before reaching the coast. By then he was virtually out of fuel so had to make a rapid landing at Rochford, Essex.

As there was a cloud-layer at 20,000 feet, the Spitfire squadrons 19 and 611 started their patrol above it. No enemy were encountered but the AA fire burst through the cloud with exciting if alarming effect. So 19 Squadron followed the Hurricane squadrons below the cloud where they met the enemy. 611 Squadron remained on patrol overhead. By the time that 19 Squadron commenced to attack, there seemed to be only one of the original two enemy groups left. This consisted of a score of bombers and some scattered Messerschmitt 110s. Bombers were mainly Junkers 88s and Heinkel 111s.

Flt Lt W G Clouston at Blue 1 fired almost all his ammunition at one of the Junkers 88s with devastating effect. The crew baled out even more urgently than usual and the Junkers crashed behind some houses to the west of Deal in Kent.

The indefatigable F/Sgt H Steere closed with a Heinkel 111 which went for the lower cloud layer at only two or three thousand feet. Steere at Blue 2 followed it down and saw it actually hit the water at the mouth of the Thames. Climbing again, Steere caught a Junkers 88 already on the dive. Green 1 had previously attacked this one and Steere finished it off. F/Sgt C H Unwin at Blue 3 closed to within 50 yards of a Messerschmitt 110. No rear fire came from it as he fired. One engine caught fire, the pilot baled out, and the aircraft crashed near Eastchurch. This was confirmed by a Spitfire of 66 Squadron.

F/O L A Haines was flying Green 1. After hitting the Junkers as already reported, he met two Messerschmitt 109s and observed firing coming laterally from one of them. It seemed to be from a fixed gun below and behind the pilot's seat. He concentrated on this aircraft and after closing to 50 yards the Messerschmitt 109 looked to be diving vertically.

Green 2 was P/O Dolezal. He took on a Heinkel on the outside of its group. Jet smoke. Spinning aircraft. The Czech saw the Heinkel spin right on down into the sea. Green 3 was another Czech. He too picked a Heinkel. By the end of his third attack, both enemy engines were stopped and the crew saw no reason to stay. They escaped. The Heinkel hit the ground near Gillingham, Kent.

Flt Lt Lawson led Red Section on nine Junkers 88 which turned desperately south-east. Red 1 fired at the rear aircraft and looked set for a success when he had to land at Eastchurch with a bad glycol leak. Red 2 attacked the same Junkers. Red 3 joined in until it was seen to crash at Sandwich. They shared the credit: P/O W Cunningham and Sgt D Lloyd. Red 4 was P/O Bradil, but the Czech could not claim any conclusive result. Nevertheless the Spitfires had done well. These were the destroyed claims of the individual squadrons: 242 Squadron, 5 Dornier 17s and 5 Junkers 88s; 310 Squadron, 5 Dornier 215s; 302 Squadron, 5 Junkers 88s, 1 Dornier 215, 1 Dornier 17; 19 Squadron, 3 Junkers 88s, 3 Heinkel 111s, 1 Messerschmitt 110. Twenty-nine enemy aircraft destroyed with scarcely a scratch. Bader had done it again!

After the devastating day success of the Wing, that night the enemy restricted their raids to several slight jabs around the Mersey area until 02.30. A couple of bombs burst on Norwich, while some of the aerodromes in East Anglia and Lincolnshire received some attention.

The raids extended into the daylight morning hours of 19 September in the Mersey, North Wales and Macclesfield locations. Across in East Anglia, mist and low rainclouds hindered any interception, the enemy diving cunningly out of the clouds, dropping their bombs and making off again. But at about 11.00 hours the weather and tactics did not deter Blue Section of 302 Section to carry out orders to climb as quickly as they could to catch a raider after it had dropped bombs near Upwood. They saw it first over Mildenhall and shot it down just north of Bury St Edmunds.

Furthermore, a Junkers 88 force-landed at Oakington completely intact but with some engine trouble. The crew appeared quite pleased to have got down safe and sound, surrendering without any fuss or resistance!

Hostile night action resembled the previous one, with industrial areas, aerodromes and docks as the main targets. There were many more high explosives than incendiaries and one bomb near Sealand made a crater 30 feet wide by 18 feet deep. On the whole it was the Mersey which bore the brunt. Slight daytime flurries during the morning over East Anglia were not continued after lunch. The Wing was actually ordered up but did not achieve any action.

The night of 20–21 September yielded raids on a smaller scale than the preceding few. The Mersey area got it again, while one or two bombs fell near East Anglia aerodromes. Almost tokens to show that the war was still on.

At 17.00 P/O D A Adams of 611 Squadron operating out of Ringway sighted a Dornier 215 from the cockpit of his Spitfire. The enemy writhed to try to get free but Adams shot it down near Hoylake: memories of peace and games of golf played down there. Then across on the eastern side of the country, the Wing were told to take off to patrol Duxford and Hornchurch. The time was 18.06 hours. They searched unsuccessfully for any action.

Night and day the war went on. Night thrusts with bombs near the hard-hit town of Warrington. Southport got some too, while fires broke out at Bootle. Two later raids signed off the night's hostility with bombs near Sheffield and Boston, Lincs. By day one enemy aircraft loosed a stick of bombs on the west side of an aerodrome. One Spitfire was destroyed on the ground there. 19 Squadron got its revenge, though, and probably destroyed the intruder. Day bombs on 22 September near Sheringham and Market Harborough.

As far as 12 Group were concerned, night bombing was restricted to East Anglia and Lincolnshire. These nuisance raids lasted on and off the entire night from 21.00 hours on 22 September till 05.45 next day, with just a couple of brief breaks. The pattern was for the raiders to cross the coast at 10,000–15,000 feet, though when nearing their allotted targets coming down to a mere 2,000 feet. Besides several near-misses on aerodromes, the following were all hit: Kirton, Digby and Waddington. More incendiaries than high explosives. A quiet day on the whole, with one raid crossing the coast at Yarmouth. Blue Section, 74 Squadron chased it out to sea but could not catch it. Sadly a Spitfire was lost together with its pilot . . . The Wing went up twice at 09.32 and 18.07 but had nothing to report.

Visual patterning of night bombing again with explosions on Liverpool, Manchester, Chester, Warrington, Widnes, Birmingham, Stourport, Huddersfield, Hull and Uttoxeter. Aerodromes were attacked too at Wittering, Digby, Mildenhall and Scampton. Bury St Edmunds received heavy treatment, while an ammunition dump was blown up at Feltwell. By contrast, the day passed inactively. 74 Squadron saw a Dornier 17 ten miles off Sheringham at 16.20 and damaged it. The Wing went up twice at 08.30 and 11.40. But only frustration, no actual enemy sightings.

Isolated raids occurred during the night of 24–25 September around the Mersey area. Bombs damaged oil-cake mills and warehouses, as well as commercial buildings in Liverpool itself. A few raiders attacked the Menai bridge with incendiaries but did not manage to hit it. The East Coast also received its quota of night intruders. Just one Wing patrol on this day, at 09.35 hours, and no contact established.

The Germans were still keeping up their brand of night and day air raids, perhaps scattered over too wide a zone for full effectiveness. A few bombs broke the night of 26 September in the north-west, while Lincolnshire had its share as well. Digby and Grantham, Sheffield and Finningley—these were four typical targets. The day-time cloud came low but bombs fell near Newport Pagnell and on Henlow camp. About 17.35 hours, a raider bombed Ellesmere Port, while another penetrated to Coventry, where bombs were dropped on Standard Motors. Motor production was suspended but aircraft manufacture was unaffected by this raid.

The date of 27 September was destined to be famous for the final large-scale Bader Wing battle in 12 Group. By night, though, the enemy estimated at 25 aircraft split up at Northwich, half for Liverpool and the rest for the Midlands. The main Liverpool to Crewe railway line was damaged and other bombs fell near Sheffield. Several fires flared up in the Liverpool dock area and damage was admitted to being extensive, with several ships hit as well.

The Bader Wing went up three times on 27 September. At 09.00 they did not meet the enemy. But at 11.42 hours the Wing was ordered off from Duxford to patrol the London area. On this occasion the Wing comprised four squadrons: 242 and 310 of Hurricanes, 19 and 616 of Spitfires.

Bader heard over R/T: 'Bandits south-east of Estuary . . . ' When he could not find them, the Duxford controller told him to return. Douglas said: 'I'll just have one more swing round.'

Turning his Wing southwards and flying at 23,000 feet, he eventually sighted enemy aircraft apparently circling around the Dover/Canterbury/Dungeness triangle at 18,000–20,000 feet. They were Messerschmitt 109s just milling around—a strange sight indeed. Visibility good with a cloud layer higher at 25,000 feet. The sun lay behind the Wing, so Douglas decided to dive into the attack. No formation attack was either possible or desirable, so having manoeuvred himself into his up-sun position he ordered the Wing to break up and attack as they liked.

Bader chose a 109 which was passing underneath him. He turned behind and above the enemy and got in a two second strike with the instant result that the Messerschmitt dissolved in thick white smoke, turned over slowly, and took a vertical dive. Others of 242 Squadron confirmed this success.

A second 109 flew in front and below him, so Douglas turned in behind. After a typical Bader burst, the 109 took evasive action by rolling on to its back and diving. Bader did the same but pulled out short and cut it off on the climb. The Hurricane had a long chase finally getting in a long distance squirt from 400 yards. A puff of white smoke slowed the 109 perceptibly. More bursts from the keen eye of Red 1. One missed completely but others hit. The last squirt produced black smoke from the port side of the enemy fuselage—and Bader's Hurricane had its windscreen covered with oil from the 109. The enemy propeller stopped dead. The last seen of the 109 was as it glided down under control but with engine dead, at a shallow angle into the Channel.

As Douglas himself was on the edge of the coast and out of ammunition after all those squirts (his favourite word), he decided that discretion was required. He dived to ground level into the haze, went back to Gravesend and landed. This last combat finished off the coast between Dover and Ramsgate. Symbolic that Douglas should be protecting his country actually over the white cliffs of Dover. Bader rearmed, refuelled, and had lunch with 66 Squadron!

But back in the air much was happening—or had already happened.

His Red 2 was P/O M K Stansfield, who chased a Messerschmitt 109 across Dover and then lost sight of it. A Junkers 88 crossed his sights so Red 2 fired a burst at about 200 yards. The enemy plodded on, smoking and turning now, flying parallel to the Kent coast eastwards. At about 50 feet from the bomber, Red 2 ran out of ammo. He did not see the Junkers 88 crash, due to the bad weather, but he felt convinced that in its damaged state it could hardly get right across the Channel from Dover.

Red 3 was Sgt P H Lonsdale, who could make no definite claims.

By Bader's standards this was turning out to be rather an unpredictable patrol, although the results were coming in nevertheless. This was because in a complete 'shambles' with everyone manoeuvring in a confined air space and the enemy on the run, the chances of scoring were far less than when a bomber group were being attacked further inland.

Bader: 'Break up and attack.'

Flt Lt G E Ball got that original message along with the rest of them. He was Yellow 1. It was noon, give or take a minute. Ball seemed to have chosen an experienced fighter pilot as adversary, but eventually he got on the 109's tail and opened fire from 200 yards. But he had difficulty in closing due to their relative speeds being virtually the same. He hit the cockpit of the Messerschmitt. But at that instant, too, Ball realised he had been hit in the tank. He was in trouble. He tried to make an aerodrome but the engine of his Hurricane started to catch fire. A few quick mental calculations and he knew he had to get down somehow–in seconds. He force-landed with the wheels still up in a field somewhere between Deal and Manston–the latter had been his goal. Denis Crowley-Milling at Yellow 2 for once had little to report, nor had Sgt G W Brimble at Yellow 3.

F/O P S Turner was Blue Leader. Behind him at Blue 2 came P/O R Bush. He found he was not in the right position to fire during that initial dive on the Messerschmitt 109s. Climbing to gain precious height again, he saw half a dozen of them about 3,000 feet above him. Not a nice sight. While Bush was still climbing to try for the rear one, their leader did a quick turn and dived on Bush. The Hurricane pilot put his aeroplane into a spin and dived, only to find one Messerschmitt 109 still after him. So he managed to conjure a quick turn and reverse their relative situations. He fired at the 109 and saw it break up in the way since familiar through the cine camera shots of the Battle of Britain. It plumed into the sea somewhere between Dover and Gravesend. Blue 3 was P/O Hart, another rare occasion when one of Bader's best men did not happen to get near enough to connect.

Green Section was the last one of 242 Squadron. P/O Tamblyn at Green 1 put his dogfight at 'Dover to mid-Channel'. As Tamblyn picked one, it throttled back and made for the sea. He found it hard to stay with the Messerschmitt. The enemy evasive tactics consisted of skidding turns, porpoising, and violent climbing turns to 500 feet. Tamblyn only shot at it as the enemy crossed his sights. The fight had descended all the way down from 12,000 feet to 100 feet! This called for desperate, precision flying. Tamblyn could see his shots hitting the Messerschmitt 109 and eventually petrol or glycol was pouring out of the fighter. Tamblyn overshot on his last burst, so could not finally claim to have destroyed the German aeroplane. He actually had 40 rounds left in one gun but a stoppage prevented him firing them. Visibility was down to a mile or even less and so, reluctantly, Tamblyn turned round for home.

F/O M G Homer at Green 2 was missing . . .

P/O J B Latta at Green 3 was at 21,000 feet and the first Messerschmitt 109 he caught at 18,000. It was doing a steep climbing turn. As Latta got within range, however, the German levelled off and received a burst from astern. It was a direct hit on the petrol tank and the enemy crashed 5–10 miles inland from Dover. That was the first of two Messerschmitt 109s which Latta destroyed.

He spotted several making for the French coast in some disarray. Still having a height advantage, Latta was able to overtake one of them and close to 50 yards. Latta's aim appeared deadly, for once again the petrol tank sparked a general fire. The enemy maintained a fairly steep dive from 10,000 feet straight into the sea, some five miles or more off Dover. Although he did not know it then, Latta's Hurricane had sustained some damage both to its tail and one wing. This must have been when he was firing at the first Messerschmitt 109. He landed at Gravesend, like Bader. The time: 13.15.

310 Squadron of Hurricanes destroyed one Messerschmitt 109. 616 Squadron of Spitfires destroyed one, too.

19 Squadron had greater opportunities and took them. Flt Lt D J Lawson at Red 1 ordered the squadron into line astern and led an attack on a large group of Messerschmitt 109s. The one he selected received several short deflection bursts and Lawson saw his tracer striking home. The enemy struggled to head for France but smoke started to be seen as it fell to an altitude of 3,000 feet. It continued its dive into the sea about ten miles out from Cap Gris Nez. Lawson was close behind it all the way and only when he was satisfied it had crashed did he turn through 180 degrees.

Sgt A G Blake at Red 2 saw a small group of 109s preparing to attack them. So he broke out of line in a right-hand turn to forestall the move. He fired at one and it turned south smoking in pale white. Red 2 fired again. The enemy then suddenly turned across his bows. Red 2 fired for the third time and the Messerschmitt hit the sea. There were other 109s speeding for home almost at sea level. Red 2 went on to attack one of those actually parallel to the surface and in the confusion the enemy pilot flew into the sea. Red 3 was P/O Bradil, who hit a Messerschmitt 109, claiming damage but not destruction.

A pair of 109s were going for Yellow Section from above. Flt Sgt C G Unwin at Yellow 1 got on the tail of one, causing it to perform dramatic aerobatics for ten minutes, trying to edge towards France. Eventually it straightened out. Yellow 1 gave it a 7-second burst from 50 yards. Still it flew. After another long and fruitless burst, Yellow 1 moved to one side and fired the rest of his ammunition at 30 degrees deflection. That really was the end. The Messerschmitt

109 stalled, seemed to hang in the air, and then spun into the sea. A worthy opponent. Another German dead.

Yellow 2 was Sgt B Jenning. He flew in fearlessly at the leader of a quintet of Messerschmitt 109s. After his attack, the enemy bowed away to starboard emitting smoke that turned from white to black. This eventually enveloped the whole aircraft. Yellow 2 could not follow it down further as he was set on by the other four Messerschmitts. Yellow 3, Sgt B G Cox had a crash and was wounded. He was rushed to hospital. Yellow 4, Sgt D E Lloyd just could not get into the circle formed by the Messerschmitt 109s. He fired some rounds but did not register any hits. Not his fault.

Green 1 took B Flight to attack eight Messerschmitt 109s. Flt Sgt H Steere opened fire from 300 yards but could not claim any successes that day. Green 2, F/O D Parrot, was about to follow Green 1 into the attack on the same aircraft when it burst into flames, so perhaps Steere should have had credit for it. Green 2 attacked another Messerschmitt 109 which went down near Sandwich. Having lost the rest of his squadron, Parrot joined with 616 Squadron for a head-on attack on other Messerschmitt 109s. Green 3, Sgt Plzak, fired at a Messerschmitt 109 and followed it from 10,000 feet, attacking all the time. From Folkestone, he saw it smoke, then flame, then dive. The end of another Messerschmitt 109.

Sqn Ldr Lane flew above the main formation and witnessed the small upper group of Messerschmitt 109s preparing to attack. He went for two of them and pulled back his stick for a second attack. His Spitfire Mark II failed to respond and he was unable to pull out of the dive until he came down as low as 3,000 feet.

Green 4, P/O Burgoyne was missing . . .

So counting the cost on both sides, the Bader Wing claimed 13 destroyed, 5 probables, 3 damaged. The individual squadron scores were as follows:—

242 Squadron, 4 Messerschmitt 109s destroyed;
19 Squadron, 7 Messerschmitt 109s destroyed;
310 Squadron, 1 Messerschmitt 109 destroyed;
616 Squadron, 1 Messerschmitt 109 destroyed.

Our losses were five aircraft damaged or missing. The pilots lost or missing were three—Homer, Smith and Burgoyne. Luckily these losses were subsequently reduced.

Duxford were delighted at the results achieved. Later on they got a message from Air Vice-Marshal Park that they had been poaching on 11 Group's preserves. Good for him, they thought—it was his way of congratulating them. Not long afterwards, Douglas discovered that this remark had been deadly serious and actually couched in the form of a complaint. Even so, Douglas was then and still is prepared to make excuses.

By October 1940, the night raids increased, the day raids diminished. Over the following month or so, the Bader Wing was ordered up about another dozen times. Yet the momentous days were already ending. Recalling September 1940, Douglas thinks it only fair to remember too that Dowding may have been considerably preoccupied in his daily contacts with the Air Staff, the War Cabinet, and indeed possibly even the Prime Minister, Winston Churchill. Under such conditions of mental stress, it is reasonable and indeed excusable that he may have been unaware of the changing circumstances of the Battle. In this case he failed in not appreciating the need for overall control from Fighter Command. He should have appointed a deputy, an Air Marshal, to co-ordinate and direct the Battle.

What has been built up into the Big Wing controversy stemmed solely from mutterings in the Mess by the pilots of the Duxford Wing against the 11 Group habit of calling them off the ground too late, so that they arrived in the battle area at a disadvantage. This was coupled with the fact that 11 Group headquarters used to complain when they were late--which was duly passed to them by 12 Group headquarters. The result was a vicious circle, with 11 Group saying that 12 Group took so long to get off the ground. Towards the latter part of the Battle of Britain matters did improve.

It should be remembered that the Duxford Wing went into action first as such on 7 September and that the big battles ceased after 21 September, so the period under discussion is only fourteen days. The difference of opinion had not been resolved by the end of the Battle of Britain. Park was opposed to the Big Wing ideas and to the general line adopted by Leigh-Mallory. Douglas found Leigh-Mallory had a quick, questing mind and a character of charm and understanding. He was tough, enthusiastic and completely honest with his juniors. He cared about people. They mattered to him. So did Douglas. Later Leigh-Mallory moved from Group Commander of 12 to 11 Group and subsequently Commander-in-Chief Fighter Command. Then as an Air Chief Marshal, he served as C-in-C Allied Air Forces Europe until he was killed with his wife in an air crash in 1944.

Douglas found him a great leader. Leigh-Mallory's career after the Battle of Britain certainly confirmed that his ideas on fighter tactics were received with considerable sympathy and agreement of the Air Council. But Leigh-Mallory and Douglas Bader have been criticised from various quarters for their attitude to fighter policy and tactics in the Battle of Britain. Now at last the minutes of a famous meeting are available as proof that the weight of opinion was with them in the Air Council. This meeting was held on 17 October 1940 and Leigh-Mallory caused a minor stir by bringing Douglas with him to such a high-level discussion. The minutes are well worth quoting in full, not only in view of the distinguished company present but also because of all the subsequent controversy over Big Wing tactics—and the way in which Leigh-Mallory and Bader were vindicated.

21. Wg Cdr D R S Bader, DSO, DFC painted by Capt Cutherbert Orde.

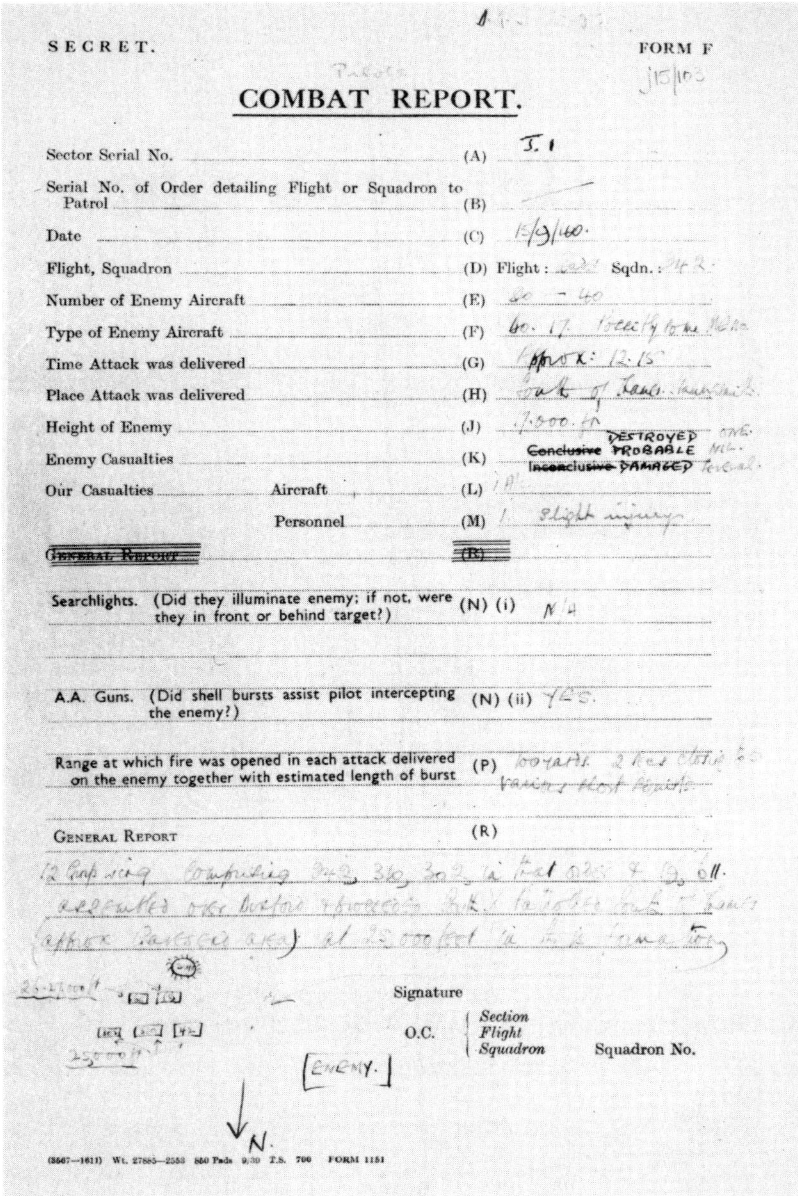
SECRET. FORM F

j15/103

COMBAT REPORT.

Sector Serial No.	(A)	J. 1
Serial No. of Order detailing Flight or Squadron to Patrol	(B)	—
Date	(C)	15/9/40.
Flight, Squadron	(D)	Flight: [illegible] Sqdn.: 242
Number of Enemy Aircraft	(E)	30 – 40
Type of Enemy Aircraft	(F)	Do. 17. possibly some Me110
Time Attack was delivered	(G)	Approx: 12.15
Place Attack was delivered	(H)	South of Thames [illegible]
Height of Enemy	(J)	17.000 ft
Enemy Casualties	(K)	~~Conclusive~~ DESTROYED ONE. PROBABLE NIL. ~~Inconclusive~~ DAMAGED several.
Our Casualties Aircraft	(L)	Nil
Personnel	(M)	1 slight injury.
~~General Report~~	~~(R)~~	
Searchlights. (Did they illuminate enemy; if not, were they in front or behind target?)	(N) (i)	N/A
A.A. Guns. (Did shell bursts assist pilot intercepting the enemy?)	(N) (ii)	YES.
Range at which fire was opened in each attack delivered on the enemy together with estimated length of burst	(P)	100 yards. 2 secs closing to [illegible] various short bursts.

General Report (R)

12 Grp wing comprising 242, 310, 302 in front & 19, 611 [illegible] over [illegible] South of Thames (approx [illegible] area) at 25 000 feet in [illegible] formation.

Signature

O.C. Section / Flight / Squadron Squadron No.

26-27000 ft 25000 ft ENEMY. N.

(3567—1611) Wt. 27885—2553 850 Pads 9/39 T.S. 700 FORM 1151

22. Combat report of Bader. His final decorations were DSO and Bar, DFC and Bar.

CHAPTER 11

A Historic Meeting

MINUTES OF A MEETING HELD IN THE AIR COUNCIL ROOM ON OCTOBER 17TH, 1940, TO DISCUSS MAJOR DAY TACTICS IN THE FIGHTER FORCE
(Reference Air Staff Notes and Agenda dated 14.10.40)

Present:—

Air Vice-Marshal W. S. Douglas	D.C.A.S.
Air Chief Marshal Sir Hugh C. T. Dowding	A.O.C.-in-C Fighter Command
Air Marshal Sir Charles F. A. Portal	
Air Marshal Sir Philip P. B. Joubert de la Ferte	A.C.A.S.(R)
Air Vice-Marshal K. R. Park	A.O.C. No. 11 Group
Air Vice-Marshal Sir C. J. Q. Brand	A.O.C. No. 10 Group
Air Vice-Marshal T. L. Leigh-Mallory	A.O.C. No. 12 Group
Air Commodore J. C. Slessor	D. of Plans
Air Commodore D. F. Stevenson	D.H.O.
Air Commodore O. G. W. G. Lywood	P.D.D. of Signals
Group Captain H. G. Crowe	A.D.A.T.
Squadron Leader D. R. S. Bader	O.C. 242 Squadron
Wing Commander T. N. McEvoy)	
Mr J. S. Orme)	

. . . .

1. D.C.A.S. explained that he was presiding at the meeting as C.A.S. was unable to be present owing to indisposition.

2. There were three propositions that he would like the meeting to consider.

(1) We wish to outnumber the enemy formations when we meet them.

(2) We want our superior numbers to go into the attack with a co-ordinated plan of action, so that the protecting fighters are engaged by one part of our force, leaving the bombers to be engaged by the remainder.

(3) If possible we want the top layer of our fighter formation to have the advantage of height over the top layer of the enemy formation.

3. This was the ideal, but it was obviously not always possible of attainment. For instance, the time factor might not allow us to do what we wanted. It might be necessary to engage the enemy before he reached some vital objective, and in such cases there might not be time either to collect a superior force or to obtain superior height. D.C.A.S. then invited comments on the propositions he had outlined.

4. A.O.C. No. 11 Group said that with the factors of time, distance and cloud that were often involved in the operations of No. 11 Group it should not be laid down as a general principle that the 'Wing' of fighters was the right formation with which to oppose attacks, even those made in mass. He felt that the satisfactory use of the 'Wing' by No. 12 Group related to ideal conditions when the enemy bombers were in retreat, separated from their escort. No. 11 Group, using formations of one or two squadrons had, on the other hand, quite recently obtained results against bombers on their way in which compared not unfavourably with those of the 'Wing' sorties from No. 12 Group.

5. The A.O.C. outlined to the meeting the principle that applied in No. 11 Group for operations against a large force of enemy bombers with a fighter screen; this involved the use of squadrons in pairs at different heights to engage separately the top fighter screen, the close escort and the bombers.

6. A.O.C.-in-C. Fighter Command said that the great problem was to obtain early knowledge as to which of perhaps many raids was the major one. The Observer Corps did good work but were often baffled by the extreme height of enemy formations. He therefore attached great importance to the development of the G.L. and L.C. organisation; Kent and Sussex would be covered by the end of November. This beam control had, of course, the disadvantage that the plot of only one formation at a time could be brought through into a Sector Operations Room, but it would be a big help when a big raid was known to be coming in.

7. A.O.C. No. 11 Group referred to experiments he had been making with reconnaissance Spitfires which, in favourable conditions, were useful for obtaining early reports of big formations. The general installation of V.H.F. would give better results from this reconnaissance work.

8. Incidentally, there had been two recent occurrences of experienced pilots on reconnaissance being shot down over 25,000 feet by raids of which the R.D.F. had given no indication.

9. Experience showed that this reconnaissance work was not suitable for young pilots whose commendable keenness led them to engage, rather than shadow, the enemy.

10. Reverting to the general question of fighter tactics, the A.O.C. said that to meet the present 'tip-and-run' raids he felt that the only safe system was that now employed in No. 11 Group. The reconnaissance Spitfire section was always backed by a strong Spitfire squadron patrolling on the Maidstone patrol line at 15,000 feet, as soon as the first R.D.F. warning was received this squadron went up to 30,000 feet and then to 35,000 feet, so as to cover the ascent of other squadrons; one of these was always at instant readiness and, generally the present situation demanded an exceptionally high degree of readiness throughout the Group.

11. A.O.C. No. 12 Group said that he would welcome more opportunities of using the 'Wing' formation, operating say from Duxford and coming down to help No. 11 Group. He could get a 'Wing' of five squadrons into the air in six minutes and it would be over Hornchurch at 20,000 feet in twenty-five minutes. If this type of counter-attack intercepted a big formation only once in ten times the effort would none the less be worth it. On two recent occasions good results had again been obtained, once against fighters alone.

12. A.C.A.S.(R) drew attention to the shortness of some of the warning that Groups had recently received.

13. A.O.C.-in-C Fighter Command said that he had recently given written orders that an 'arrow' should go down on the Operations Table on receipt of the first 'counter'; it must be realised that the enemy's approach at great height presented a difficult problem.

14. A.O.C. No. 11 Group said that he could face the problem when it was a large bomber raid that was coming in. Could it not be accepted that if his Group had, say, twenty squadrons at readiness, that was generally sufficient to meet any enemy formation?

15. Discussions followed on this question and it was generally agreed that additional fighter support would often be advantageous since the more we could outnumber the enemy, the more we should shoot down. The A.O.C.-in-C said that he could, with his Group Commanders, resolve any difficulties of control involved in sending

such support. The other main difficulties to be met, it was agreed, were those involving the time factor, though in this connection it was mentioned that the Me.109 carrying bombs had not, so far, been found over 22,000 feet.

16. Squadron Leader Bader said that from his practical experience time was the essence of the problem; if enough warning could be given to bring a large number of fighters into position there was no doubt they could get most effective results.

17. Air Marshal Portal enquired how much a local concentration might affect the responsibility of a Group Commander for the defence of all the area of his Group. A.O.C. No. 12 Group said that satisfactory plans were prepared to meet the possibility of other attacks coming in; he was satisfied that the concentration of a 'Wing' was not incompatible with his general responsibility as Group Commander.

18. This raised the question of whether some of No. 12 Group's squadrons might be moved to No. 10 Group which was the C.-in-C agreed at present somewhat weak should any concentrated attack develop in the West. On the other hand, the protection of the Midlands and of the East Coast convoys was a big commitment for No. 12 Group. Though it was a serious limitation he had, as C.-in-C to keep in mind the necessity of meeting every threat with some force.

19. Further discussion followed in which the importance of a long warning from the R.D.F. was stressed. A.C.A.S.(R) said that everything was being done to get the south-east coast R.D.F. stations back to full efficiency following the damage suffered from enemy attacks. He mentioned the recent example when a twenty-five minutes steady R.D.F. warning had not been received without delay in No. 11 Group. It was decided that No. 11 Group should have the services of a certain member of the Stanmore Research Station who had previously been of assistance to them.

20. D.C.A.S. said he thought the views of the meeting could be summarised as follows:

> The employment of a large mass of fighters had great advantages, though it was not necessarily the complete solution to the problem of interception. In No. 11 Group, where the enemy was very close at hand, both the methods described by A.O.C. No. 11 Group and those of A.O.C. No. 12 Group could on occasions, be used with forces from the two Groups co-operating.

21. The A.O.C.-in-C said that it would be arranged for No. 12 Group 'Wings' to participate freely in suitable operations over the 11 Group area. He would be able to resolve any complications of control. In reply to D.H.O. the C.-in-C. said that co-operation of this kind could, in the present circumstances, hardly be employed generally throughout the Command as similar conditions seldom arose elsewhere.

22. With reference to the formal Agenda prepared for the meeting, the following observations were made:—

Items 1 & 2

Items 1 and 2 formed the subject of general discussion as shown above. It was agreed that where conditions were suitable, wings of three squadrons should be employed against large enemy formations and that where further forces could be made available without detriment to other commitments larger fighter formations than Wings should operate as tactical units.

It was agreed that it would, on occasion, be convenient to operate two Wings together as a unit and that, for want of a better name such a unit should provisionally be known as a 'Balbo'.

Item 3

It was agreed that it would not always be practicable to operate the combined squadrons of a Wing from the same aerodrome, particularly in winter when aircraft might be confined to the runways. It was, however, agreed that all the squadrons of a Wing should operate from the same Sector.

Item 4

It was agreed that, as was now the practice, the Wing or 'Balbo' should be controlled by the Sector Commander. It was considered undesirable for a squadron Commander from one of the squadrons to control such a formation.

Item 5

No major difficulty was foreseen in co-ordinating the operations of the two Wings of a 'Balbo'; it was agreed that one Sector Commander should control the two Wings and that when possible the two Wings of a 'Balbo' could work on a common frequency.

Item 6

It was agreed that, in the conditions which enable the enemy to operate in mass formation, the fighter leader could dispense with sector control and that if he was given information about enemy movements he should be responsible for leading his formation to the battle.

Item 7

It was agreed that all squadrons of a 'Balbo' could operate effectively on the same frequency with H.F. R/T and that by using V.H.F. a theoretical maximum of seven 'Balbos' could be operated.

It was agreed that when V.H.F. R/T was introduced the method of working suggested in paragraph 13 of the Air Staff paper would be satisfactory.

Item 8

It was not thought that Wings could be regarded as permanent units to be moved complete, but that whenever possible the same squadrons should operate together as a Wing.

Item 9

It was agreed that where practicable, Wings should be deployed at stations from which they could gain advantage in height over the enemy without having to turn.

Item 10

23. A.O.C.-in-C., Fighter Command, in amplification of his earlier Reports, gave the meeting an interim account of the development of the A.I. Beaufighter. As yet, troubles with the Mark IV A.I. the Beaufighter, and its engines, were causing much unserviceability, but he was satisfied that the system was sound in principle.

24. The method of using searchlights in clumps promised good results and was about to be developed in the South.

25. D.C.A.S. and D.H.O. referred to the grave problem of maintaining civil morale in London, in the face of continued attack, over the two or three months that might be expected to pass before the system outlined by the C.-in-C. was practically efficient. To bridge the gap during the intervening period it was suggested that a temporary Wing of two Defiant and two Hurricane squadrons should be formed to specialise in night fighting on a 1914–1918 basis. C.-in-C Fighter Command said that continual experiments had been made on these lines, many of them by the A.O.C. No. 10 Group who had, since the last war, been a specialist in night interception, but with the height and speed of modern night raids the old methods had not so far proved effective. He felt certain that now the only sound method would be a combination of A.I. and G.L. (or L.C.); his Defiant squadrons were, however, now being normally employed on night interception. While it was his considered opinion that the

diversion of Hurricanes to night interception was a dangerous and unsound policy, with our present strength of Fighter Squadrons, he had nevertheless agreed with reluctance to implement the Air Staff decision to do so. These aircraft he felt, might show reasonable results in clear weather when the controlled clumps of searchlights began to work round London towards the end of November, but a real solution to the problem would only be found through the logical development of a system based on the two new radio aids to interception.

26. A.O.C.-in-C. said that he would be prepared to experiment with a 'Fighter Night' over London, but this was not a course he could recommend. As people heard the fighters over London they would imagine that the noise represented so many more enemy aircraft, and the experiment would be justified only if it were successful.

27. A preliminary draft of the scheme which D.C.A.S. and D.H.O. had explained to the meeting was handed to the C.-in-C. Fighter Command who undertook to examine it.

★ ★ ★

Although the Battle of Britain may already have been won, neither the rest of the conflict nor even the war in the air generally were over—and 12 Group suffered several tragic losses at this late phase. While Douglas was in London on the very day of 17 October, Red Section of 242 Squadron got orders to orbit base at 08.40 hours. And though instructions were given to pancake, these were cancelled and at 09.07 hours Red Section received a vector. Flying at a height of about 7,000 feet about 09.15 hours, they saw a Dornier 17 cruising on a course some 3,000 feet below. Visibility at 7,000 feet was good but at 3,000–4,000 feet there was 8/10ths cloud. When first sighted the Dornier was making for a dense cloud.

They were 30 miles north-east of Yarmouth as Red 3, P/O B A Rogers, attacked from above and to starboard of Red 2. Red 3 got in a good burst. Then Red 2, P/O M N Brown, positioned himself dead astern of the enemy bomber and also got in a burst before experiencing fire from the enemy rear gunner which connected with his throttle control. Red 2 was followed in line astern by Red 1, P/O N N Campbell. Red 2 saw nothing further of Red 1 before breaking away. When he returned to attack, the enemy had vanished into the cloud and Red 2 made back to base.

Red 3 followed the Dornier 17 through a succession of clouds, catching occasional glimpses of all or part of it. But he failed to close in for a further effective burst and finally lost it altogether. When last seen by Red 3, the Dornier was still proceeding at a fairly slow speed on an easterly course in no apparent difficulties. Red 2 landed at 09.50. Red 3 landed at 10.20 hours. Red 1 failed to land. P/O N N Campbell was posted as missing.

On the very next day the Polish Squadron 302 suffered still more severely. Operating with 229 Squadron, they were told to scramble at 15.00 hours in poor weather and patrol Maidstone line at Angels One Five. Twelve fighters were airborne by 15.06 hours. They joined up with 229 Squadron over the base, 302 leading. After one or two varied manoeuvres and various vectors, Flt Lt Jathomson at Red 1 espied an enemy. He turned towards it and attacked three times. The first was from behind slightly above. The second and third followed vertically from above. During the first attack he met heavy enemy fire from four machine guns, two of them in the rear gunner's turret. The other two guns were located in 'blisters'. Many Hurricanes were also attacking enemy aircraft at the same time so he broke off to avoid collision. His bandit scampered into the clouds pursued by several Hurricanes. Red 2 attacked unsuccessfully. Red 3 was unable to fire at any enemy as he could not manoeuvre into position.

Yellow 1 was likewise unsuccessful. Yellow 2, Sgt Nowakiewicz closed on the enemy from 150 to 30 yards. He broke away on a climbing turn after a burst. As he did so he saw two men jump from the enemy and two parachutes open just afterwards. The aeroplane dived gently towards earth. Yellow 3 could not position himself for an assault but confirmed the two parachutists.

No pilots in Blue or Green Sections who returned were able to attack successfully.

After the initial attack, the squadron reformed and Yellow 2 said that he was the last aircraft in the squadron. He counted ten others besides himself. The leader asked for his position and was told he was 30 miles from base at 16.26 hours.

The leader thinks he lost the last three sections when descending to Angels Five to investigate badit reported at that altitude at 16.30 hours. At 16.46 he asked for permission to land as he had been up for 1 hour 40 minutes. But he was told to orbit for two minutes as another bandit was nearby. Red Section eventually landed at Northolt at 17.08 hours.

The fate of the other sections was as follows:—

Blue 1 landed at Cobham with one gallon of petrol left in his tank.

Blue 2, P/O Wapniarek, crashed at Cobham. An eye-witness said he saw four aircraft flying overhead very low in and out of cloud. One of these aircraft detached itself and seemed to shut off its engine. A moment later it came out of the cloud and crashed, catching fire immediately.

Blue 3, P/O Zukowski, crashed and was killed near Detling.

Green 1, F/O Carter, and Green 2, F/O Borowski, both crashed at Kempton Park Race Course within 200 yards of each other.

Green 2 and Yellow 3 both landed safely.

So four pilots were killed: Carter, Wapniarek, Borowski and Zukowski.

Equally tragic to Douglas Bader were the later losses of pilots from his original Canadian 242 Squadron. On 5 November, P/O N Hart, to be followed by two others, P/O J B Latta and P/O Willie McKnight. Douglas Bader remembers these men always. They were the immortals of The Few. And a lot of other men remembered Douglas from those days—and to this day. Opinion is still very mixed over the question of Big Wing tactics and it may be interesting to quote three or four Battle of Britain pilots on this question, and also on their memories of Douglas as he was in 1940.

Johnnie Johnson: 'Douglas was a well-established figure and a squadron leader when I came in as a pilot officer. Everybody had heard about this almost legendary chap, even in those days. I first met him in August 1940. My own squadron 616 had been pulled out of the front line. Half the squadron had been lost or wounded. We went back to Coltishall to re-form. Douglas was there with his Canadian squadron. Here was this legendary chap with his tough Canadians. We had an invasion scare on Saturday evening. Everyone was getting in a terrible panic with rumours of impending German landings. Douglas just walked into the mess and said, 'We'll give them the squirts—jolly good show' and calmed things down at once.

'Douglas was all for the Big Wings to counter the German formations. I think there was room for both tactics—the Big Wings and the small squadrons. The size of the fighting unit in 11 Group was conditioned by the time to intercept before the bombing. It might well have been fatal had Park always tried to get his squadrons into 'Balbos', for not only would they have taken longer to get to their height, but sixty or seventy packed climbing fighters could have been seen for miles and would have been sitting ducks for higher 109s. Also nothing would have pleased Goering more than for his 109s to pounce upon large numbers of RAF fighters. Indeed Galland and Mölders often complained about the elusiveness of Fighter Command and Park's brilliance was that by refusing to concentrate his force he preserved it throughout the Battle. This does not mean, as Bader pointed out at the time, that two or three Balbos from 10 and 12 Groups, gaining their height beyond the range of the 109s, would not have played a terrific part in the fighting. Park only had time to fight a defensive battle. The Balbos could have fought offensively. This was a matter for Fighter Command.'

Peter Townsend: 'Bader is a very great person, but of course he was involved in a highly controversial thing and in the judgment of many—and occasionally in my own judgment—he did infringe the rules. But I've let that be known in a very friendly way. He even visualised control of squadrons should have been handled from Fighter Command, even by Dowding himself. When I put this to Park, he said, "Well, I must say, that beats the band."

'Sholto Douglas thought it "ideal" if Park's squadrons could attack the incoming bombers, with Leigh-Mallory's Wings harrying them as they retreated. Douglas Bader's idea was exactly the opposite: operating only from 12 Group or the flanks of 11 Group, Wings should take off and gain height as the enemy was "building up" over France, and then advance in mass to attack them as they crossed the coast. Meanwhile, 11 Group squadrons climbing from forward airfields beneath the fray would tear into the retreating enemy. Bader never thought wings could operate from 11 Group's forward airfield.'

Peter Brothers: 'There was a lot to be said for this big wing conception if they could be marshalled in time. But it obviously wouldn't work in 11 Group. But it could work in 12 Group. I flew in both Groups. Of course later on in the Battle, one was organised in big wings. You had that little bit more time to play. There was something to be said on each side. Park was quite right that it wouldn't work in 11 Group—they were too far forward. There was certainly a case when you were further back for a large formation.'

Alan Deere: 'I first met Douglas during Dunkirk operations, when I was operating at Hornchurch and he came down. When I first met him, I didn't know about his legs. I walked into the mess. I can remember very distinctly. He was standing near the hatch where we got our drinks. He struck me at once in the way he attacked you, came at you. I met him and at that point I hadn't even heard of him before. He kept pumping me about tactics and shouting and all this sort of thing. Immediately he stood out as someone who was keen to get on with the job and wanted to find out all about it. That was in May 1940. I was shot down during those Dunkirk operations and don't recollect talking to him again at that time.

'I heard about him during the Battle of Britain, because of these wing tactics which are now so much in controversy. All I will say is that tactics will always remain a matter of opinion. But it is my opinion that the mass wing formations of 12 Group could not have been successful in 11 Group. There just wasn't time to form up and get airborne. For example, when we were operating from Manston—the most forward airfield in 11 Group—we actually had to fly inland to get our height before we could go back to meet the raids.'

But of course Douglas Bader did not advocate big wings from Kent or Surrey. And he did advocate an offensive attitude to the defence of Britain. No-one can prove him finally right or wrong, but he had certainly scored substantial successes—for the minimum losses. Then in the following spring and summer, he really went over to the offensive, and as Johnnie Johnson says: 'His greatest qualities came to the fore . . .'

Air Chief Marshal Sir Trafford Leigh-Mallory, KCB, DSO, shown later in the war as Allied Commodore in Chief under General Eisenhower.

24. About to take-off, the celebrated Supermarine Spitfire Mk I with its Rolls-Royce Merlin II engine.

25. Battle of Britain flypast in September 1945: Air Chief Marshal Lord Dowding with pilots before they took off from North Weald. Group Captain Bader, who led them, is in the centre.

CHAPTER 12

Over to the Offensive

In March 1941 Douglas Bader was posted to Tangmere, Sussex, as wing leader of what soon became known as the Tangmere Wing. He was the RAF's very first wing leader and the three squadrons he commanded were 616, 610 and 145. Many of his lasting friendships dated from that spring and summer, which culminated in his crash over France on 9 August. The flavour of these days can be conveyed by the impressions of some of those friends—and then the sorties themselves. But first, the friends.

Johnnie Johnson: 'We went on to a wing of three squadrons which was about right. The great thing was that previously we had been fighting a defensive battle. Then we began to reach out and take on the Luftwaffe over the Pas de Calais. There Douglas's greatest qualities came to the fore: leadership, the ability to inspire, and his great desire to get out and at them. It was quite extraordinary. Something I had never known before or have never known since. The qualities of moral courage, the ability to command, and the fact that he spoke the same language as these chaps. I was still a pilot officer. Douglas was a wing commander. I think I had reached the elevated ranks of flying officer when he crashed in August. We were all rather like his pupils. Like master and apprentice. He always went to great lengths to have a post-mortem afterwards and explain things to us. Everyone loved him.

'Tactically, because the enemy abreast formation was better than the astern pattern, Fighter Command lagged behind the German Fighter Arm. It was not until this spring that Douglas Bader copied the Schwärme, which he called the "Finger-Four" because the relative positions of the fighters are similar to a plan view of one's outstretched fingertips. Bader's pilots were immediately impressed with their finger-fours, for, unlike the line astern pattern, all pilots were always covered, and all stood an equal chance of survival. Soon all fighter squadrons followed Bader's lead. It had taken a long time to relearn the doctrine of Oswald Boelcke.'

Laddie Lucas takes up this theme, as an observer rather than a participant in 1941. 'As I see it, every pilot in the RAF owed something to what went on in World War I. These tactics were used again, by ourselves and by the Germans. But the actual line abreast flying, the basic concept of a pair of aircraft, or four aeroplanes in the form of a finger-four formation—these were fundamental tactics whether used in World War I, by the Spaniards, or the Germans, or whoever else. The fact of it was that Douglas modernised it, brought it up to date, made it fresh and practical for flying in the 1940s. And don't forget, this was in direct conflict with a lot of the flying thinking that was being done in 11 Group, which was all line astern. It was quite all right to climb a squadron or a wing up in line astern to battle height, but then so often they stayed together like that and never came up to line abreast. Terrible for the junior pilots at ass end Charlie. Douglas started with the basic two aeroplanes, then the finger four, then the fours in touch with one squadron, two squadrons, three. This was the basis, with two pilots looking inwards, so that the whole sky was covered right through 180 degrees. This was really fundamental to all his flying, both defensively and offensively, in the sweeps over the north of France from Tangmere. Douglas never claimed to have pioneered the technique.' Some people have criticised these tactics as being old hat—but nothing could be further from the truth.

Hugh Dundas takes it one stage further: 'Douglas was very much a pioneer in getting away from that line astern formation. In fact he and I conducted an experiment together, following a long conversation in the mess. We tried a bit of finger-four and adopted it. I certainly never flew anything else for the rest of the war. We were flying over France all the time now, instead of over England. We were doing sweep after sweep after sweep, all day, every day. We always flew in fours. I flew as the other leader, next to him. We did over sixty sweeps together that summer before he crashed. He liked to have the same chaps with him. He was a hell of a help to me. I had a very nasty bit of being shot down in 1940. I was shot down and couldn't get out of the aeroplane. The hood stuck. The aeroplane stopped flying. I got out very low indeed at about three or four hundred feet. I was only on the end of a parachute for three or four seconds. That shook me considerably. I think if I hadn't come up against someone like Douglas, I might have found it very difficult to get going again. He was a great leader. He liked his wide circle of friends. We used to go to his house and we spent most of that spring and summer together, one way and another.'

Douglas and Thelma Bader lived in a modern house near Bognor with a big window. Bay House was five or six miles from Tangmere and its doors remained always open to anyone at the station. Thelma's sister Jill lived with them. Once or twice a week Johnnie Johnson would drive over to Bay House, to find the hard core of the Tangmere Wing grouped about its leader. Stan Turner was invariably there. He had been with Douglas in 242 Squadron, of course. Douglas sipped his lemonade, analysed their recent flights, and discoursed on the importance of straight shooting. Meanwhile the sorties were stepped up. It became a strange contrast between high summer, high clouds, the scent of clover, and even an odd game of golf at Goodwood–and then the sudden sweeps over France. The electric trains purred on: Chichester, Barnham, Ford, and so to Brighton. Thelma and Jill looked after Bay House and were always cheerful. And the Tangmere Wing flew on. The Bader Wing. As 'Cocky' Dundas said, sweep after sweep after sweep. The years of 1940 and 1941 called for greatness. Douglas supplied it.

Nothing can completely recapture the flavour or strain of *sixty, seventy* Spitfire sorties in two or three months. So here are just ten typical combat reports from 21 June to 23 July told in Douglas Bader's own words:–

21 June 1941

'I was leading Tangmere Wing which was milling around in and off the coast around Desvres. Saw the bombers and escort go out near Boulogne, followed by AA bursts. We stayed around above and behind the bombers and escort when I noticed two Messerschmitt 109s in line astern about to turn in behind my section of four. I told them to break left and twisted round quickly (metal ailerons) and fired a very close deflection burst at the first Messerschmitt 109E at about 50 yards' range, about ½ to 1 second. My bullets appeared to hit him as his glass hood dispersed in pieces and the aeroplane pulled up vertically, stalled and spun right-handed. I foolishly followed him down with my eyes and nearly collided with a cannon Spitfire of another squadron in the Wing and then reformed my section. I claim this as destroyed (a) because I know it was and (b) because F/O Marples 616 Squadron saw a Messerschmitt 109 spinning down at the time and place and Sqn Ldr Turner of 145 Squadron saw a pilot bale out of a Messerschmitt 109 at the time and place, as also did one of his pilots, (c) F/O Machatek of 145 Squadron saw a Messerschmitt 109 dive into the sea right alongside another Messerschmitt 109 which had been shot down by one of 145 Squadron, same time and place, and (d) no-one claims the second 109 which I am sure was mine.

25 June (a.m.)

'I was the Tangmere Wing Leader flying with 616 Squadron and taking off from Westhampnett at 11.58. Joined up with 145 and 610 Squadrons and proceeded up over Dungeness at 20,500 feet. Then flew on to a point opposite Gravelines and turned straight towards coast, flying south. Noticed a number of Messerschmitt 109s from time to time above and what looked like a combat in the Gris-Nez/Boulogne area at 25,000 feet. When 145 Squadron informed me that they had found bombers and were escorting bombers back over Gravelines, I gave the order for the Wing to withdraw. As we crossed coast at Gravelines at about 18,000 feet my section ran into 4–6 Messerschmitt 109Fs milling around over Gravelines–Dunkirk area about 500 feet below. We flew into them and I gave one a short deflection shot and my No 2 (Sgt West) followed in with another burst of two seconds. Sgt West broke to port and lost sight of enemy aircraft but I broke to starboard and saw it half roll and dive down and followed it down–giving it ½ second burst–seeing pilot baling out about 5 miles off Gravelines in sea. Then vectored 280 degrees from this point, crossed over South Foreland and returned at Westhampnett at 13.35. This Messerschmitt 109 was not visibly damaged although bullets were seen to strike: i.e. no smoke etc.

25 June 1941 (p.m.)

'As Tangmere Wing leader and flying with 616 Squadron, we took off from Westhampnett at 15.49 and joined up with 610 and 145 Squadrons. Climbed up to 21,000 feet and crossed French coast at Hardelot(?). Joined up with bombers underneath and then flew east with them for a few minutes when numerous enemy aircraft were seen behind, below and to the north of us. Eventually was compelled to engage them and disregard the bombers, since they were all round us and we were flying down sun. With the leading section I engaged 8 to 9 Messerschmitt 109Fs which were climbing east to west, i.e. towards Boulogne. We were then at 20,000 feet and the enemy aircraft between 16,000 and 17,000 feet. We dived on to them and F/O Dundas and his No 2 attacked two who turned north and climbed. I attacked four Messerschmitt 109Fs, with my No 2, who were climbing in a slightly left-hand turn. I gave a short burst at one at close range from inside the turn and saw white, black and orange-coloured smoke envelop the aircraft, which went down in an increasingly steep dive which finished up past the vertical. I did not follow the aircraft down and claim it as destroyed. I straightened up from turn just as some more Messerschmitt 109s (which were milling about some Spitfires) turned towards me. I gave a short head-on burst on one of them, who I don't think had seen me, but saw no apparent result of my fire. I then joined up with Sqn Ldr Holden of 610 Squadron with my No 2 and gave a burst at another aircraft but saw no result. Landed Westhampnett at 17.22.

2 July 1941

'I was leading 616 Squadron's first section. Sighted approximately 15 Messerschmitt 109Fs a few miles south-west of Lille so turned south and attacked them. They were in a sort of four formation climbing eastwards. They made no attempt to do anything but climb in formation so I turned the Squadron behind them and about 200 feet above and attacked from behind. I attacked a Messerschmitt 109F from quarter astern to astern and saw his hood come off—probably he jettisoned it—and the pilot started to climb out. Did not see him actually bale out as I nearly collided with another Messerschmitt 109 that was passing on my right in the middle of a half-roll. Half-rolled with him and dived down on his tail firing at him with the result that glycol and oil came out of his machine. I left him at about 12,000 feet, as he appeared determined to continue diving, and pulled up again to 18,000 feet. My ASI showed rather more than 400 mph when I pulled out. Found the fight had taken me west a bit so picked up two (610 Squadron) Spitfires and flew out at Boulogne round Grisnez and up to Gravelines where we crossed the coast again and found a Messerschmitt 109E at 8,000 feet at which I fired from about 300 yards. No damage but this one is claimed as "Frightened"! The first Messerschmitt 109 is claimed as destroyed since, although I did not actually see the pilot leave the aircraft, I saw him preparing to do so, and several pilots in 616 saw two parachutes going down one of which was shot down by P/O Heppell. The second Messerschmitt 109 was seen by P/O Heppell and is claimed as damaged.

4 July 1941

'Intercepted one Messerschmitt 109E some miles south of Gravelines at 14,000 feet, while with a section of four. Turned into its tail and opened fire with a short 1-second burst at about 150 yards. I found it very easy to keep inside him on the turn and I closed up quite quickly. I gave him three more short bursts, the final one at about 20 yards' range and as he slowed down very suddenly I nearly collided with him. I did not see the result except one puff of white smoke halfway through. Sqn Ldr Burton in my section watched the complete combat and saw the Messerschmitt 109's airscrew slow right down to ticking-over speed and as I broke away the Messerschmitt 109 did not half-roll and dive—but just sort of fell away in a sloppy fashion, quite slowly, as though the pilot had been hit. Having broken away I did not again see the Messerschmitt 109 I attacked, since I was engaged in trying to collect my section. I am satisfied that I was hitting him and so is Sqn Ldr Burton from whose evidence the above report is written. This Messerschmitt 109 is claimed as a probable.

6 July 1941

'During the withdrawal from Lille to Gravelines we were pestered by Messerschmitt 109s starting to attack and then half-rolling and diving away when we made to engage. Of an initial three bursts I fired at three Messerschmitt 109Es I claim three frightened (P/O Johnson subsequently destroyed No 3). Finally, two Messerschmitt 109Rs (I think) positioned themselves to attack from starboard quarter behind when my section was flying above and behind the bombers south of Dunkirk. These two were flying in line astern and I broke my section round on to them when they were quite close (250 yards away). They both did a steeply banked turn, still in line astern, and exposed their complete underside (plan view) to us. I gave one a short burst (no deflection) full in the stomach from 100–150 yards and it fell out of the sky in a shallow dive, steepening up with white and black smoke pouring from it, and finally flames as well. The pilot did not bale out while I was watching. This is confirmed by P/O Johnson and Sgt Smith in my section, and is claimed as destroyed.

9 July 1941

'Just after crossing French coast (with bombers) at 18,000 feet I saw a Messerschmitt 109 behind and above me diving very steeply, obviously intending to get down below and behind bombers and attack from underneath and then zoom away. I instructed my section I was diving down, and dived straight through and under the escort wing converging on this Messerschmitt 109 who had not seen me. He saw me as he was starting his zoom and turned right-handed, i.e. into me, and dived away. I was very close by then and aileroned behind him and gave him a 1–2 second burst from 100–150 yards straight behind him. Glycol and heavy black smoke streamed out of his aeroplane and he continued diving. I pulled out at approximately 10,000 feet and watched him continue downwards. When he was about 2,000 feet I lost him and then saw a large flash on the ground where he should have hit. I am sure it was him but I am claiming a probable only because when flying out over the same terrain I noticed sun flashes on glass in various directions, and as I did not actually see the 109 right into the ground these sun flashes must be recorded. Just after leaving the target area my section was attacked from above and behind and we turned into the attackers, Messerschmitt 109Fs, who started half-rolling. I got a good short squirt at one and the glycol stream started. Did not follow him down and claim a damaged. Several others were frightened and I claim one badly frightened who did the quickest half-roll and dive I've ever seen when I fired at him.

10 July 1941

'Was operating in a four over the Béthune area at 24,000 feet when we saw five Messerschmitt 109s below us in a wide loose vic. We attacked diving from above and I opened fire at one at 200 yards closing to 100, knocking pieces off it round the cockpit and pulling up over the top. I saw flashes as some of my bullets struck (presumably De Wilde). Was unable after pulling up to see it again, but saw and attacked without result three of the same five (so it is to be supposed that two were hit), immediately after pulling up and turning. My own aeroplane shielded my view immediately after the attack and I claim this one as a probable only, because of the incendiary strikes and the pieces coming off the cockpit.

'Was flying with section of four northwards over 10/10ths between Calais-Dover. Sighted three Messerschmitt 109Es below flying south-west over the cloud. Turned and dived to catch them up which we did just over Calais. The three Messerschmitt 109s were in line abreast and so were my section with one lagging behind. I closed in to 150 yards behind and under the left-hand one and fired a 2-second burst into its belly under the cockpit. Pieces flew off the Messerschmitt 109 exactly under the cockpit and there was a flash of flame and black smoke, and then the whole aeroplane went up in flames. This was seen by Sgt West and P/O Heppell of my section. Time approximately 12.50. Height 7,000 feet. Position, south of Calais or over Calais.

12 July 1941

'When orbiting the wood at Bois De Dieppe about to proceed to St Omer at 26,000 feet, we saw approximately 12–15 Messerschmitt 109Fs climbing in line astern from Dunkirk turning west and south. I told my section we would attack and told the two top squadrons to stay up as I thought I had seen more Messerschmitt 109s above. We turned so that the enemy—who were very close and climbing across our bows—were down-sun, and I fired a very close deflection shot at the second last one at 100–50 yards' range. I saw De Wilde flashes in front of his cockpit but no immediate result as I passed him and turned across him and fired a head-on burst at the last

Messerschmitt 109 who had lagged a bit. A panel or some piece of his machine fell away and he put his nose down; as I passed over him I lost him. I then turned round 180 degrees to the same direction as the 109s had been going but could not see them. I called my section together and, after a little, made contact with them. I then saw the Bee Hive and bombers flying over the St Omer wood travelling south-east just below with a squadron of Spitfires above. I saw two Messerschmitt 109Fs above the Spitfires and dived down to attack. These two flew away south more or less level and I closed up quickly on one which I shot from 100 yards dead astern and produced black smoke and glycol. The second one was banking to the left when I attacked the first and he dived a little after the first. I got in behind him with a good burst, followed him through 10/10ths cloud (about 100 feet thick) and gave him one more burst which set him on fire with a short quick flame under the cockpit, then black smoke, then the whole machine caught fire round the fuselage. The pilot did not bale out. I pulled away at 9,000 feet and I reckon this aeroplane crashed between St Omer and Béthune. I went up to 14,000 feet and called my section together, they were both above the cloud in the same area, and we had no more combat. I believe they had a fight at the same time. Of the four Messerschmitt 109Fs one was definitely destroyed and the other three are considered damaged. The one which disappeared through the cloud layer emitting black and white smoke I consider was more likely a probable.

23 July 1941

'Took off from Manston with Sqn Ldr Burton at approximately 13.40 after 242 Squadron on the expedition to bomb ship off Dunkirk. The weather was very hazy from about 1,000 feet upwards but clearer below. We flew from North Foreland and near Gravelines and were attacked by a Messerschmitt 109 out of the sun. We countered and Sqn Ldr Burton had a shot at it. It flew low over the water to the French coast.

'We carried on up to Dunkirk and slightly past where we saw some flak and then a Spitfire (squadron markings XT) flying straight for home in a dive being attacked by a Messerschmitt 109. We immediately turned on the Messerschmitt 109 which saw us and did a left-hand climbing turn back to France, but I got a very close short burst (½ second) at him from underneath and behind him. It definitely hit him and produced a puff of white smoke under his cockpit. I turned away immediately as I had no idea how many were about and did not want to lose Sqn Ldr Burton. I claim this Messerschmitt as damaged but would like confirmation from 242 Squadron who told me on landing back at Manston that they had seen two Messerschmitt 109s go into the sea in that area. We flew back to Manston after this and landed amongst 242 Squadon, who arrived back at the same time. I claim a damaged aircraft just around Dunkirk out to sea, which may be a destroyed one. I never saw this Messerschmitt after breaking away but the visibility was poor.'

Although Douglas Bader would have been the last to admit it, he must have been beginning to feel the strain after 1940-41—a year's operations and a century of sorties. In the final phase of July/ August 1941, he led ten sweeps in seven days. Then came 9 August. He was leading the Tangmere Wing escorting RAF bombers on a raid on France. He was now flying a Spitfire VB and the time was about 11.00 hours. First of all, Bader takes up the story of the morning—written by him nearly 4 years later:

'We crossed the French Coast south of Le Touquet with bottom squadron 616 at 26,000 feet and 610 Squadron above. The Wing had lost 41 Squadron after take-off. Attacked a climbing formation of about twenty Messerschmitt 109Fs. I told 610 Squadron to stay put, and dived with my section on to the leading four Messerschmitts. "Come on, boys, there are plenty for all. Pick one each." I nearly collided with the first one at whom I was firing, and had to go behind and under his tail. Continued downwards where I saw some more Messerschmitt 109s. I arrived among these who were evidently not on the look-out, as I expect they imagined the first formation we attacked were covering them . . .'

What happened next is best described by Paul Brickhill in his immortal Bader story, *Reach for the Sky.*

Paul Brickhill:

'He was suddenly surprised to see six more Messerschmitts ahead, splayed abreast in three parallel pairs line astern, noses pointing the other way. More sitters! He knew he should pull up and leave them; repeatedly he'd drummed it into his pilots never to try things on their own. But the temptation! They looked irresistible. A glance behind again. All clear. Greed swept discretion aside and he sneaked up behind the middle pair. None of them noticed. From a hundred yards he squirted at the trailing one and a thin blade of flame licked out behind it. Abruptly a flame flared like a huge match being struck and the aeroplane fell on one wing and dropped on fire all over. The other Germans flew placidly on. They must have been blind.

'He aimed at the leader 150 yards in front and gave him a three-second burst. Bits flew off it and then it gushed volumes of white smoke as its nose dropped. The two fighters on the left were turning towards him, and crazily elated as though he had just pulled off a smash and grab raid, he wheeled violently right to break off, seeing the two on that side still flying ahead and that he would pass between them. In sheer bravado he held course to do so.

'Something hit him. He felt the impact but the mind was curiously numb and could not assess it. No noise but something was holding his aeroplane by the tail, pulling it out of his hands and slewing it round. It lurched suddenly and then was pointing straight down, the cockpit floating with dust that had come up from the bottom. He pulled back on the stick but it fell inertly into his stomach like a broken neck. The aeroplane was diving into a steep spiral and confusedly he looked behind to see if anything were following.

'First he was surprised and then terrifyingly shocked to see that the whole of the Spitfire behind the cockpit was missing: fuselage, tail, fin—all gone. Sheared off, he thought vaguely. The second 109 must have run into him and sliced it off with its propeller.

'He knew it had happened but hoped desperately and foolishly that he was wrong. Only the little radio mast stuck up just behind his head. A corner of his brain saw that the altimeter was unwinding fast from 24,000 feet.

'Thoughts crowded in. How stupid to be nice and warm in the closed cockpit and have to start getting out. The floundering mind sought a grip and sharply a gush of panic spurted.

"Christ! Get out!"

"Wait! No oxygen up here."

"Get out! Get out!"

"Won't be able to soon. Must be doing over 400 already."

'He tore his helmet and mask off and yanked the little rubber ball over his head—the hood ripped away and screaming noise battered at him. Out came the harness pin and he gripped the cockpit rim to lever himself up, wondering if he could get out without thrust from the helpless legs. He struggled madly to get his head above the windscreen and suddenly felt he was being sucked out as the tearing wind caught him.

'Top half out. He was out! No, something had him, the leg holding him. (The rigid foot of the right leg hooked fast in some vice in the cockpit.) Then the nightmare took his exposed body and beat him and screamed and roared in his ears as the broken fighter dragging him by the leg plunged down and spun and battered him and the wind clawed at his flesh and the cringing sightless eyeballs. It went on and on into confusion, on and on, timeless, witless and helpless, with a little core of thought deep under the blind head fighting for life in the wilderness. It said he had a hand gripping the D-ring of the parachute and mustn't take it off, must grip it because the wind wouldn't let him get it back again, and he mustn't pull it or the wind would split his parachute because they must be doing 500 miles an hour. On and on . . . till the steel and leather snapped.

'He was floating, in peace. The noise and buffeting had stopped. Floating upwards? He thought, it is so quiet I must have a rest. I would like to go to sleep.

'In a flash the brain cleared and he knew and pulled the D-ring, hearing a crack as the parachute opened. Then he was actually floating. High above the sky was still blue, and right at his feet lay a veil of cloud. He sank into it. That was the cloud at 4,000 feet. Cutting it fine! In seconds he dropped easily under it and saw the earth, green and dappled, where the sun struck through. Something flapped in his face and he saw it was his right trouser leg, split along the seam. High in the split gleamed indecently the white skin of his stump.

'The right leg had gone.

'How lucky, he thought, to lose one's legs and have detachable ones, otherwise he would have died a few seconds ago. He looked, but saw no burning wreck below—probably not enough left to burn.

'Lucky, too, not to be landing on the rigid metal leg like a post that would have split his loins. Odd it should happen like that. How convenient. But only half a leg was left to land on—he did not think of that.

'He heard engine noises and turned in the harness. A Messerschmitt was flying straight at him, but the pilot did not shoot. He turned and roared by fifty yards away.

'Grass and cornfields were lifting gently to meet him, stools of corn and fences. A vivid picture, not quite static, moving. Two peasants in blue smocks leaned against a gate looking up and he felt absurdly self-conscious. A woman carrying a pail in each hand stopped in a lane and stared up, frozen like a still. He thought—I must look comic with only one leg.

'The earth that was so remote suddenly rose fiercely. Hell! I'm landing on a gate! He fiddled with the shrouds to spill air and slip sideways and, still fumbling, hit, feeling nothing except vaguely some ribs buckle when a knee hit his chest as consciousness snapped.'

— Paul Brickhill

Meanwhile Tangmere had no idea of what had happened to Douglas. In the hectic moments of that fight, no-one had noticed his sudden disappearance, no-one saw the collision. Woodhall was the controller at Tangmere. At the end of the sortie, he called over the air:

'Douglas, are you receiving?'

There was no answer.

Johnnie Johnson called the group captain:

'We've had a stiff fight, sir. I last saw the wing commander on the tail of a 109.'

'Thank you, Johnnie,' the group captain replied courteously.

When they landed, they found out that Douglas and Buck Casson were both missing. Johnnie Johnson and Cocky Dundas were two of the pilots who almost at once asked for permission to return and try to find them. They did so, but without trace.

It was about teatime on that summer afternoon. Thelma and Jill were at Bay House, as they had been so often that summer, awaiting Douglas's return. Instead the intelligence officer arrived from Tangmere.

Thelma was sitting in a deck-chair in the garden. 'Hello, John. Come for tea?' The name of the young officer was John Hunt. He thought that Thelma already knew about Douglas and became so embarrassed about it that he could not bring himself to tell her. Quite understandable, in view of the intense feeling and affection Douglas had generated. Neither Thelma nor Jill could make head or tail of him. Then Woodhall arrived.

'Oh, look, here's Woodie,' Thelma said.

As soon as they met, she could tell by his face that something was wrong.

'I'm afraid I've got some bad news for you, Thelma. He hasn't come back from the morning sortie.'

Jill Lucas was also there. She felt the physical sensation of that moment. The sense of shock. As if one's heart had stopped. But Thelma and Jill had both been convinced that Douglas was absolutely invincible; that the Germans would never get him.

Thelma was quite calm about it. At least, externally. She sat down. She must have visualised the possibility of such a moment despite all her hopes.

Woodhall went on: 'Of course, we're all looking for him and I hope we'll hear something very soon. We'll let you know the moment there's any news.'

Then he left. They were very quiet for a while. There was almost nothing to say. Then Jill noticed that for the only time she could ever recall, Thelma just could not cope with the cooking. The next few days were going to be bad.

This is what Johnnie Johnson said:

'We, too, were silent when we drove to the mess, for we knew that even if our wing leader was still alive he would have little chance of evading capture with his tin legs. Before this, we had rarely thought of his artificial limbs, and it was only when we swam together and saw his stumps and how he thrashed his way out of the deep water with his powerful arms that we remembered his infirmity. At Tangmere we had simply judged him on his ability as a leader and a fighter pilot, and for us the high sky would never be the same. Gone was the confident, eager, often scornful voice. Exhorting us, sometimes cursing us, but always holding us together in the fight. Gone was the greatest tactician of them all. Today marked the end of an era that was rapidly becoming a legend.'

As soon as Douglas was taken to hospital, he asked his captors to search for his other artificial leg. He suggested that it would still be in, or near, the remains of the aircraft. In case it was not, he also asked if the Germans would signal to England requesting delivery by air of his spare right leg. This, in company with his spare left leg, was in his locker at Tangmere. To his surprise, the Germans acceded to both wishes. Within a day or two, the Germans retrieved and mended the missing leg.

Thelma thought Douglas was alive, but began to get more and more worried as she felt that the Germans would be bound to announce it if they had Douglas–as he was such a capture. Yet she still felt it was out of the question that he could be lost.

The boys from Tangmere told Thelma and Jill: 'You'll have to face it. He won't come back. One of us would have seen something.'

Jill had an absolutely certain conviction that Douglas was still alive. He *felt* alive to her. She had never been so sure of anything. So she said to the boys:

'Well, I don't believe you.'

Jill used to lie awake at night thinking of Douglas and willing him to be alive. Thinking how lonely he must be out there. She wondered where he was. By then she thought that Thelma had really begun to believe he might be lost. The boys used to come down and try to take them out for a drink. It was awful trying to go on as if nothing had happened.

Days dragged appallingly.

Eventually Woodhall was able to broadcast the welcome news on the Tangmere Tannoy: 'Attention all ranks. This is the station commander speaking. You will all be pleased to know that Wing Commander Bader is alive and well on the other side of the Channel. He is a prisoner of war.'

They had heard from the International Red Cross that Douglas was in hospital at St Omer and the Germans had offered safe conduct for a small aircraft to fly to France and take a spare set of legs.

The phone went in Bay House, telling Thelma and Jill that this message had been picked up on the radio. After they heard the news, they went out with the boys and had a tremendous party.

A little later on, a number of British aircraft in the course of a normal operation swept across St Omer airfield. As the last of them had streaked away, a long yellow box was seen floating down on a parachute. Surviving the attention of the German gunners on its descent it reached the ground, where it was found to be addressed to the Commandant of the airfield for transmission to Wing Commander Douglas Bader, DSO, DFC. The box reached Douglas. It contained, of course, his spare right leg from Tangmere.

After a spell in hospital at Frankfurt, he was then imprisoned in several camps before finally reaching Colditz Castle, near Leipzig. He was there nearly 3 years.

Yet even while in captivity, Douglas and his example were helping to win the war. The Tangmere pilots remembered those sixty-odd sweeps; that calm, matter of fact leader; his complete control; the voice that never rose an octave higher; and more than anything else, the tactics he taught them.

Laddie Lucas went out to Malta in the early part of 1942. He sailed out with Stan Turner of 242 Squadron and also from Tangmere. They got to Malta on a shimmering-blue Mediterranean morning. They were just going into the mess for breakfast when the air raid sirens started to sound. The place had been hammered to hell. At that moment, four Hurricanes flying in line astern climbed away, like whiting eating their own tails. Stan Turner looked up and said:

'Jesus Christ! They're sure not going to fly like that with me.' In the Tangmere Wing led by Douglas, Stan Turner was squadron commander. Douglas, Woodhall and Turner had developed the finger-four into what was required in the early middle part of the war.

Stan Turner became Wing Commander Flying at Malta. He came to fly with 249 Squadron, when Laddie Lucas was a flight commander. Stan Turner told them:

'Well, I don't know what you fellows have been flying. I saw four Hurricanes flying around yesterday morning line astern. I don't like that. No-one's going to fly line astern around here any more, because I'm interested in *living*. This is what we flew with Bader at Tangmere, and that's what we're going to fly here. And if there are any of you who don't like it—there are plenty of ways out.'

Some very quizzical faces looked back at the tough Canadian. But he was determined they would fly this way. The direction that Stan Turner gave them in the air, coupled with the first-class commentary and controlling from Woodhall combined to enable them to win the rest of the Battle of Malta—by a Tangmere team plus a few others.

Later on Laddie Lucas was posted to RAF Coltishall to command the fighter wing there. SASO 12 Group told him: 'We've lost three wing commanders in three weeks, Lucas, and I want you to understand that you've been sent here to stop the rot. We can't have it.'

Lucas saw that they were flying line astern, so he said at once, just as Stan Turner had done on Malta and Douglas had done at Tangmere: 'We're going to fly line abreast here. We won the Battle of Malta this way.' The casualty rate was substantially reduced and the wing commander survived.

So the practice of flying line abreast was one of Douglas's achievements. It became fundamental to a great area of flying in the Royal Air Force. In fact the fighter tactics Douglas developed spread fast and far. And when Denis Crowley-Milling got his own squadron, he modelled it on all he had learned from Douglas's squadron and wing. Crowley-Milling formed his first Typhoon squadron, fittingly at Duxford. Then he went into 83 Group and had a squadron and later a wing of Typhoons in the 1942–43 phase of the war. An apt sequel to the story of Douglas Bader, 242 Squadron, the Bader Wing, and the Battle of Britain.

Index

Please note that one or two small inconsistencies exist in the names and initials appearing in this book particularly among the personnel of Polish and Czech Squadrons.